Awful Presentations

Why We Have Them and How to Put Them Right

Barry Brophy

DARK
RIVER

Published in 2017 by Dark River, an imprint of Bennion Kearny Limited.

ISBN: 978-1-911121-31-2

Published by Dark River, an imprint of Bennion Kearny Limited
6 Woodside
Churnet View Road
Oakamoor
ST10 3AE

Cover image by Hamza El Gehani

ABOUT BARRY BROPHY

Barry Brophy has nearly two decades experience helping people make presentations in both the private sector and as lecturer at University College Dublin. There he has developed specialist Masters courses that run across all disciplines in the university and has carried out research on how oral presentations work and what gets remembered. He is also the author of *The Natural Presenter – Turning Conversations into Presentations*, which was published in 2007.

CHAPTERS

CHAPTER 1

Reading Off the Slides – Bullet Points and More Bullet Points

The Problem

I could show you many examples but do I really need to? We have all experienced this problem, probably hundreds of times. People fill slide after slide with bullet points and then read them out, one by one. You know you're in trouble when you catch a glimpse of the slide-sorter at the start of the presentation, and it looks like an aerial view of the American Great Plains: lots of dull-coloured rectangles, each intricately lined. Not only does it resemble ploughed prairie, it is about as interesting.

CONCLUSIONS

For -20, -20°C, capacity arrives to maximum at 1000 rpm and then is constant not affecting COP-total.

Power of Compressor increases with fan speed due to the increase of mass flow rate.

Coefficient of Performance decreases below 1000 rpm due to the increase of the compressor power.

For 0, 0°C, fan speed affects total capacity, but at 700 rpm we don't reach set point in room 1, and occurs up to 1500 rpm, so it's better to work only at high speeds for this compressor pack.

Fan speed variation can causes a COP peak at 2000 rpm and then decreases due to a drop in total capacity.

The all too familiar text-laden, bullet point slide.

This is bad for the audience – who wants to read text, or have it read to them(?) – but it is worse for the presenter because he or she gets sucked into gawping at their own slides to remember what they were going to say. And it's actually even worse than this because a bullet point-driven presentation is indicative of an encyclopaedic approach – point; sub-point; sub-sub-point – which is totally unsuitable for a short, transient, audio-visual communication. And, apart from being ineffective, it is also a missed opportunity to use more visual content that will excite curiosity and make your points easier to understand and memorable. It's a bad idea all round.

The Reason

The million dollar question is why on earth do people do this? Repeatedly. If you look for a precedent in popular culture you won't find one. The only time text is overlaid with someone talking is when subtitles are used in films and this is only done when the audience doesn't speak the language of the film (obviously). Subtitles are typically made as unobtrusive as possible so as not to detract from the interesting pictures that the audience actually wishes to see.

If you search the education and psychology literature, again you won't find evidence that on-screen text aids verbal delivery. In fact, the field of *Cognitive Load Theory* throws up many studies that say the exact opposite: text is distracting, not enhancing, and certainly not appealing. But it doesn't take a rocket scientist or a cognitive psychologist to work this out. Try reading a book and having a conversation at the same time; it can't be done.

In my experience there are three reasons why people persist in filling slides with *bullet points*. None are good reasons, but because presentations are so presenter-centred – with presenters worrying far more about what they are saying than what the audience is hearing – these three factors dominate thinking during the preparation phase.

Firstly, bullet points act as a prompt for the presenter. This is helpful to the speaker but not the audience. Why would they want to see the speaker's guide notes? Also it leads the presenter into a damaging cycle. The more text you put on the screen, the more you need to read that text to remind you what you put there in the first place. The act of having a prompt begets the need for one, if you think about it.

*The more you put on the screen, the more you have to look at the
screen to remember what you put there.*

The most extreme example of this I have encountered was a philosophy PhD student who, at conferences, favoured reading his paper out, word for word. This is actually the norm in many of the humanities disciplines. He told me that his argument was so intricate and required such precise explanation, that he had to write it down in a very ordered way or he would lose his train of thought. The obvious counter-argument to this is that if he needed such a precisely crafted script to allow him, the expert, to follow his own argument, then what chance had the audience got of following it?

The second reason for bullet points is that people plan their presentations in PowerPoint. Often I hear presenters say things like, 'Well, I have ten minutes, so that's ten slides: three on company background, one each on our five products, and two to wrap up.' This approach can only result in a brain-dump of bullets and not a well-structured presentation.

To be honest, I can understand why it happens. A presentation is like an exam: you prepare and worry about it for maybe weeks on end, but the second before you start to speak – just like the second before you turn over an exam paper – you still have nothing to show for your efforts. Everything may yet go wrong. No matter how many times you run through the presentation in your head, those words keep sliding around mercurially and coming out differently. The worry is that when you get up to speak, they won't come out at all. By writing these words down on slides, you're latching them in place. Now you can be sure that the presentation will progress in a precise order which is greatly reassuring. The only downside is, your presentation will be awful.

The third reason for this hail of bullets is the increasing tendency for companies to use PowerPoint 'slide decks' – a term I abhor, by the way – as documents. 'Email me the PowerPoint,' is an expression you often hear and suggests that the presentation should work nearly as well *without* the presenter. The irony being that the 'slide deck' is usually the least interesting part of that presentation.

So if you look at these three reasons for bullet points you'll realise that they perform functions before, during, and after the presentation. Before the presentation, PowerPoint is a plan; during the presentation it is a prompt; afterwards it is a document. But although these are valuable aids to the presenter, none benefit the audience. And you could probably throw in a fourth reason why people fill their slides with text: they see other people doing it! Which, as hopefully this book will show, is the worst reason of all.

The Solution

The solution is simple.

1. Get rid of the text, or nearly all of it.
2. Figure out how to overcome the challenges – planning, prompting, documenting – that bullet points are normally used for.
3. Find something good to put on the slides instead. We'll come to that.

1. Decluttering

Getting rid of the text is not difficult and although it may be traumatic, like decluttering your kitchen, it will be a weight off your mind. Delete all the text. In fact, delete the entire file, close PowerPoint and take out a blank sheet of paper. This is where you begin the planning process.

2. Planning, Prompting, Documenting

Next write down an aim for your presentation in one sentence. This is where the presentation will take your audience and this will be your conclusion. Think of the presentation as the justification of this conclusion. Let's say you have spent four months working on a project, then your conclusion might be:

Recommendation for future direction of project…

or

Get agreement/decision on…

or

Prompt audience to ask questions about…

Then you can build the content around this end point. We will look more closely at how you do this in chapter 4 on structure, but for now take it that having a clear plan makes the choice of relevant visual aids much easier. The key thing is to separate your plan from your slideshow. The slideshow should be like a salesman's carpet-bag of samples which you dip into when you need something to help you make a point.

Now you have a plan, what should you use as a prompt to keep you on track during the presentation? Creating helpful guide notes can be tricky because if there is too much written on the sheet, you won't be able to pick up where you left off; but if you have too little written there, the instructions might, in the heat of the moment, be enigmatically brief.

'*Next steps.*' What steps?

'*Show example.*' Example of what?

The best solution I have found to this problem is to make your notes as visual as possible. An example from one of my own talks is presented below and you can see that along with the one- or two-word cues, there are images, symbols and different colours to distinguish different types of content: red for demonstration, black for slides, green for examples, etc.

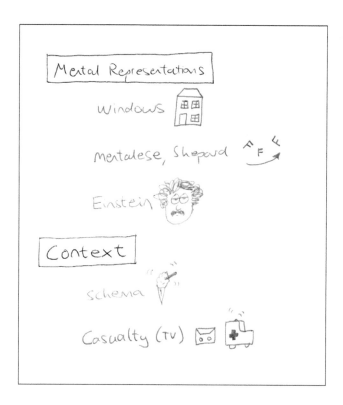

Pictures, particularly ones you drew yourself, are an excellent prompt because their meaning is more concise and immediate than a string of words. The above prompt sheet is from one of my own presentations.

There remains the question of handouts. What do you leave the audience with after the presentation?

It is difficult to form a coherent record of a short fleeting presentation and I have come to realise that the audience will tie many of their memories to the visuals you showed them. You will notice this in the Q&A at the end where there will be questions like, 'Remember the diagram you showed with the orange arrows on it...' or, 'Can you return to the photo of the building, the one with the flags in front...'

So, your actual slideshow is a useful memory hook for the people who witnessed it, but it doesn't stand on its own as a document. Which is a problem, as your presentation can take on a life of its own after you have given it. If you have presented to a client and presented well, then the recipient of that presentation will often relay the key messages to other people in their organisation. 'That guy who came in to us last week was very interesting,

I'll dig out his slides.' So it makes sense to give your audience something coherent to bring to the next stage. But what?

A friend of mine, John Dunne, who started his own company in digital telecoms, faced this same problem. John is a superb presenter and revealed a slideshow he created on a very un-straightforward concept called 'optical packet switching'. For this, he used chopped up pieces of colouring pencil, a hand-drawn sketch of a ring network and a step-by-step slide animation that brought a very complex concept to life in an accessible way. The audience loved John's presentation, but with only drawings and no text, how could they use this creative slideshow in follow-on meetings with co-workers, to relay what they had heard?

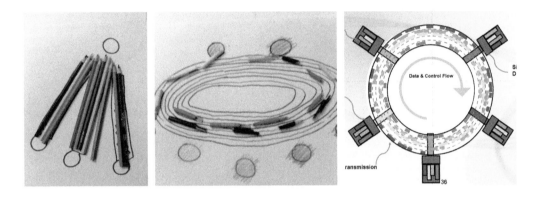

These samples are from a creative slideshow on 'optical packet switching'. Left and centre are animated slides made from photographs of pieces of colouring pencil, and on the right is the video animation this description builds towards.

'The problem,' said John, 'is that the people you present to will use that presentation internally to sell after you've gone. So the temptation is to put essay-like information into the presentation so that it becomes a reference document. But of course that is completely counterproductive on the day.'

'So, what did you do?' I asked him.

'We started by having two presentations, and we would add notes to one. But very often, when the notes were passed on, the guy who read the presentation didn't read the notes, or didn't tell their colleagues that the notes were there. In the end, we came up with a simpler solution. We'd mix information slides with picture slides and skip the information slides on the day. But we would give the customer a glimpse that they were there. It provided the comfort that, tomorrow, they wouldn't need to explain the diagram themselves.'

Simple and effective. And it's interesting that John saw the overall problem as about creating notes, not a problem with creating slides. The visual-ness of the slides was never compromised. There is no point having great notes if you have lousy slides because the presentation won't enthuse people enough to look at those notes afterwards.

3. What to Put on the Slides

I have three simple rules for this:

- Use images, not text.
- Show one thing at a time.
- Make items full-screen if possible.

Images not text. I have talked about this point, already. Text is not a visual aid. Period. But you may notice a contradiction here. I have used bullet points in the list above, and I would probably do the same thing if I were talking about this in a presentation. So there are times when a brief list of points can be useful, particularly to anchor a presentation.

You may return to this list periodically to show your progress through the presentation.

If you are doing this, though, try to make each item in the list readable in one visual fix. Many people are not aware of the fact that when you read a paragraph of text, your eye doesn't scan smoothly across the page like a child running a finger under every word. Instead it jumps to two or three locations in the line and reads a cluster of words together. So if you can make the phrase just one eye-fix long, it will be more punchy. If bullet points run longer than this, many people won't read them.

Bullet points are really just headings to talk around. The side-by-side examples below show a typical set of bullet points on the left and a much clearer, equally coherent set on the right.

<table>
<tr><td>• Production cycle times reduced by 11%.</td><td>• Time ⬇ **11.0 %**</td></tr>
<tr><td>• Material costs increased by 5.5% (€44.07/unit).</td><td>• Cost ⬆ **5.5 %**</td></tr>
<tr><td>• Current packaging system unsuitable – alternative may lead to changes in overall cost.</td><td>• Packaging **??**</td></tr>
</table>

In the bullets on the left, you will notice how the key numbers get camouflaged by the text surrounding them, whereas on the right they stand clear. There is nearly always redundant text in bullet points and you should try to remove as much of this as possible.

The other thing I have done is to align the numbers and add a place of decimals to the first figure, 11.0%, to make it consistent with the second, 5.5%. This makes the numbers look more like what they mean, and again makes the conclusion stand out. The arrows accentuate the conclusions as does the addition of colour – green for improvement, red for worsening – to add a further layer of emphasis.

In an effort to make bullet points clearer, the tendency of presenters is to add more words but actually you are making them less clear by doing this. You are hiding the key point in a bramble of redundant text. You have to remember that what you say – with the added emphasis given by eye contact, hand gestures, facial expressions and a strong voice – will be far more powerful than what you write down. Only the key pieces of information should appear in the bullet points, the explanation of these can be achieved by the most important visual aid of all: *you.*

Show one thing at a time. Consider the slide below. This was taken from an actual presentation and although the words and images have been changed, the format is exactly as per the original.

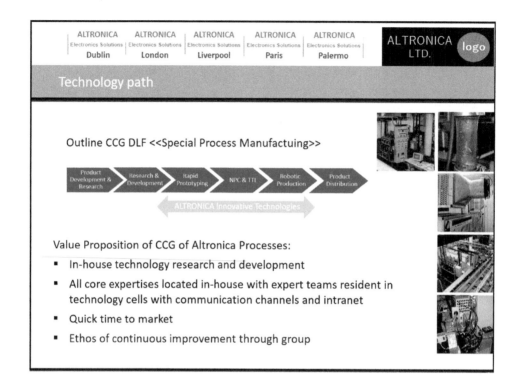

This is not an extreme example for me to ridicule; this is typical. It came from a series of presentations I attended, and to put it into context I have shown (below) exact replica slides from the next two presentations in the same workshop. As you can observe, all are similarly dense and intricate.

ELECTRICO : Electronic & Production Specialists
<< Key Technologies >>
from ideas to products

- Laser Doppler Anemometry
  - Doppler radiopropegation
  - Bextis, TFCC...

- Specialist Equipment: Remote environment equipment
  - In-house type-K thermistors
  - Long-life telemetrics
  - Integrated system with thermal sensors and dissipative heat sinks and packs
  - Severe HEM environment

- Specialist Equipment: Harsh environment equipment
  - Piezoelectric charge amplification and dissipation pre-amplifiers
  - Impedance matching and high resistance low-drift senors

- Front end Adaptive Control (ccm)
  - Proportional & integral control
  - Differential modification
  - Adaptable gain setting

- Remote Chip Isolated Control
  - Embedded control and full DSS portability
  - Analysis functions from remote PC

- ACC for battery in-the-field tests
  - Light weight high power control up to 100 V
  - Even power distribution for 85% battery life

- Calibration for 2 years with auto remote re-calibration
  - Certified to ISO standard

Company Name
logo

04 July 2017 -
Barry Brophy CEO, Dublin
Company Outline:

Design:
Arithmetic Logic Unit (ALU™)
> 100 technologies
> Memory banks, Logic, Analog

Purchase Partners :
LMA CCD - Dublin
FHH - Galway

Product Design BCC:
Smartflex/Secure BCC
Low pressure
Smart speaker system
BB-SQRL

Innovation Clients:
Element Pico Mechatronics
Panther Automation
JPAC

Finance:
€134M cash raised
Committed Group

Management team:
70 employees
>>300 Associated Partners

Sales Plan

	Cost	Charge	Total
2017	€54M	€12M	€66M
2018	€72M	€15M	€87M
2019	€82M	€17M	€97M

The first problem is that there is far too much content on all of these slides. For example, on the third slide, there are 67 words, 18 numbers and 8 images. That's a total of 93 items. Each item represents a visual instruction: look at me. That's 93 visual instructions! Each slide above was only one of three slides in a five-minute presentation, so in under two minutes, you are issuing 93 visual instructions which is a colossal over-reach. And, in fact, there are more than 93 pieces of content on this slide because when people see items side by side, or listed, or tabulated, they start to make comparisons and look for trends. This is really what tables and lists are supposed to prompt people to do; otherwise why group them at all? So there upwards of a hundred visual instructions on this one slide.

Information overload is not the only problem, though. Let us go back to the slide we first showed and examine the images. If we highlight one, in the bottom right-hand corner, and make a rough calculation of its area (which you can do with the on-screen 'guides' in PowerPoint) it can be seen to occupy just $1/51^{st}$ of the total area of the slide. So it is effectively 51 times smaller than it could be.

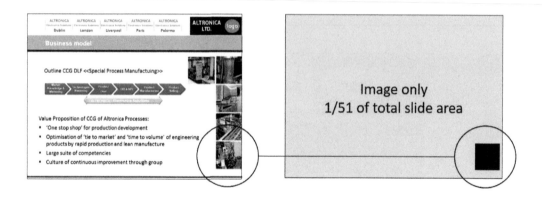

This has two implications. First – obviously – it is much harder to see than it needs to be. Second, nestled amongst many other elements, it is impossible for the viewer to know in what sequence to view it. By having just one item per slide, you are imposing a visual logic which can really clarify what you are saying.

In turn, within a given slide, you can use simple animations to make things appear, grow, grey-out or disappear in harmony with your verbal delivery. Used with restraint – and only to serve your message: no rounds-of-applause sound effects or bouncing word-swirls, please – these tools allow you to create clear, powerful visual arguments.

Whether you are animating a diagram within a slide, or showing a gallery of images across slides, try to make the images as large as possible and introduce them one-by-one.

Make images full-screen where possible. This follows on from the last point – one thing at a time – but goes a little further. Companies often insist on their employees using in-house templates when making a presentation. These have pre-defined spaces for inserting bullet points and sub-points, and perhaps a box for inserting an image or a graph. The slides also have a company logo and contact details, and possibly some background design or water-marked image to reinforce the brand. They don't look too bad, generally, but when projected onto a screen, they kill the energy of the central image by telescoping it and surrounding it with scrappy decorations.

The side-by-side slides shown below demonstrate this point but don't do it full justice; for that you would have to see the slides projected onto a large screen. In that setting, a high-resolution image – easily taken on your phone or obtained online – can look truly cinematic. It is crazy to curtail the potency of strong images, particularly when none of the other information on the slide is doing any communication work. As one of the guest lecturers on my courses, Paolo Carbone, says, 'Having a company template on every slide is like handing the audience your business card and introducing yourself every two minutes.' It's unnecessary. Don't do it.

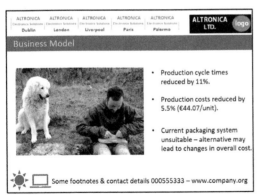 

Templates, borders, logos and unnecessary text on slides, apart from reducing the size of images, telescopes them and diminishes their impact.

You may, however, think comments like these are unhelpful. If your boss tells you to use the company template and I tell you otherwise, who wins the argument? Who's paying your wages? Fair enough, but you can work around silly in-house directives like this quite easily.

You can still use the company template but make the image so large that it just so happens to run to edge of the slide and cover the template behind it. A little accident of formatting, you could call it. The point is, no one in the audience will notice what they haven't seen, even your boss. A gallery of images is just that: a gallery of images. The audience will engage with those images as you are talking about them and that will be their sole focus. Likewise, if you showed them a demonstration, they would only be viewing what's in your hand or what you pass around, and there's no company template around that. So who cares if they don't see the template on every slide; who even notices? Just be sure, that the template *does* appear on your introduction, conclusion and key signposting slides, and you'll be fine.

 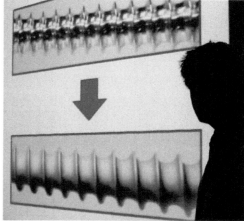

The screen often dwarfs the presenter and although you should never let the slideshow take over, it provides an opportunity – slides and presenter together – for a spellbinding interactive show-and-tell.

Many companies actually go further and have a full set of slides which they demand their employees use. You are instructed to give the stock company presentation. This is a truly woeful idea. Wretched! A stock presentation, given by anyone, will be interesting to no one. It is no different from getting employees to learn, verbatim, a script for one-to-one meetings with clients. It stems from a desire to control the message and keep employees within bounds, and in this regard it works. The problem is, no one will listen to it.

This actually hits on a universal truth that I will return to several times in this book, which is this: *communication is a creative process*. There is no one sentence or definition or script you can read out that will magically implant your ideas directly into the minds of your listeners. The topic may be as old as the hills but the audience will vary and so will the context in which you are communicating it. Everyone is different and everyone has a different personality and a different set of experiences and stories to tell. The examples, analogies, demonstrations, and pictures you use (or more accurately, you should use) will vary with you, your audience, and with what is current. Electronics, medicine, economics, biology, business: the discussions around these and all other topics change by the month.

You can observe this in conversations. Often, a speaker will try to find the best way to communicate something. 'How do I explain this? Let me see. Oh, yeah, think of it this way...' We scurry about, mentally, in search of the most pertinent examples or analogies or stories or images that will make what we are saying clear. We seek to make connections from our mind to the mind of the listener, and these connections change with every new conversation.

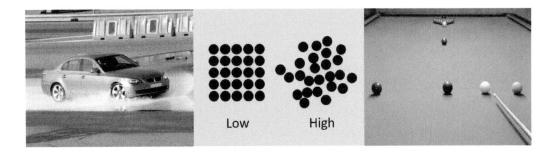

Three visual examples to explain the concept of 'entropy'
(see explanation below). However I saw none of these when I was
studying engineering in college, only equations and diagrams.

As an example, above are three images I have used in lectures to explain entropy. Without getting bogged down on the concept, entropy can be thought of as the 'quality' of energy.

We all know that energy is never created or destroyed, but as it changes from one form to another, it can lose quality.

The image on the left of a car braking is an example of this, as ordered movement-energy is changed to disordered heat-energy, which is basically jiggling atoms. The central image relates to the idea of order and disorder, which is another way of explaining entropy. The snooker table on the right is a more tangible idea of the order-disorder explanation although maybe I could swap this for a pool table if I were presenting to an American audience.

So although the concept of entropy is two hundred years old, the way you explain it changes with the context of the presentation and with time. There are a thousand ways to explain anything and you need always to be mindful of this and not just go with the first thing that comes into your head. You are not speaking to a room full of you. And just as the way you explain things changes with every new audience, so too will the slides you use. An inflexible stock company presentation, therefore, is a disaster. Don't use one.

Pictures

We have looked at slide design in general but, to finish this chapter, I want to look more closely at what the main component of these slides should be. Pictures!

What really brought this home to me was a set of presentations I attended, two years ago, given by a group of statisticians. Although extremely professional, the presentations were a little dry. Like so many talks, there was information overload in the form of text, equations and diagrams that were neither very engaging nor easy to understand.

Then, half-way through the session, a woman got up, plugged in her laptop and a splash of colour filled the screen. It was like an impressionist painting – it may well have been an impressionist painting – and when it appeared, full-screen and without any text, someone in the audience exclaimed: 'Woo!'

I thought, because the presenter was working in the area of data analytics, that this was some sort of software visualisation of a large data set. But it wasn't, it was just her screensaver. A few seconds later the impressionist painting was replaced with a dull PowerPoint slideshow and the presentation began.

This story may not seem like much but it stayed with me. Firstly, the biggest reaction of the day was for a screensaver. That tells you something about the dullness of the slideshows you normally see. Secondly, it brought home to me that you cannot tell the eyes of audience members what to like. Your eye will be drawn to something before you become consciously aware of what it is. Why work against this perceptual predisposition? Your slides should be relevant to your topic, of course, but why can't they be visually arresting as well?

Many presentations contain no pictures and, in doing so, fail to utilise the real power of images which work on three levels. First, they grab attention, as the colourful screensaver did. Second, they aid comprehension which is the 'thousand words' idea we are all familiar with. And third, they are memorable. Sometimes an image will stay with you long after the content, or even the presenter, has been forgotten.

Even the most erudite broadsheet newspapers use images liberally.

The counter-argument to this is that a serious presentation is no place for gimmicky images. You are there to inform, not entertain. Wrong! Yes you are there to inform but the simplest way to do this is by working with the audience's visual preferences, not against them.

There is nothing frivolous or gimmicky about the use of appropriate images. Even the most erudite broadsheet newspapers have 30-40% visual content, primarily images. There is nothing light or trivial about the news stories these papers feature, but for engagement, comprehension and memory, the images help. The same goes for online sources; glancing at the BBC website at the time of writing, there isn't a single headline that is not accompanied by an image, and within each article there are an average of 4-5 further images or graphics.

Presenters sometimes worry about 'overloading' their audience with images but cognitively this is not a concern. From the moment you wake in the morning until the moment you close your eyes at night, you take in a ceaseless stream of video and audio information. Listening and seeing simultaneously is easy. Listening and reading, on the other hand, is impossible. Filling slides with bullet points doesn't work.

It is so straightforward, nowadays, to put pictures into a presentation. You can either take these pictures yourself or search for them online. They should always be relevant to your talk, but there is enormous scope to bring a visual angle to your ideas. Even if the audience has seen what you are describing before, there is great merit in showing a clear image in relation to the new insights you are presenting. People will regard that image with new eyes when you tell them something fresh about it.

Just a pot of honey, from a presentation on honey.

I remember a very vivid example of the power of simple images in a presentation on the threat to the honey bee. There were full-screen, high-resolution images of bees gathering nectar from brightly coloured flowers and one picture which simply showed a pot of golden honey. The presenter even had a jar of honey on the table in front of him. The audience was fully engaged but everyone had (probably) seen honey before and tasted it. The subject matter was familiar but the audience was learning new insights and that made the familiar seem spellbinding. This presentation brought home to me how simple images and simple demonstrations can be so powerful, and certainly much better than a wall of text.

I could go on but I won't. It's very simple: *visual aids* should be *visual*.

CHAPTER 2

Being a Hologram –
Not Making Eye Contact

The Problem

If you have lots of text on your slides, as discussed in the last chapter, you'll end up reading it. But presenters without much text on their slides can often end up reading that as well.

What do I mean?

Well, when I replay videotaped presentations to people, they are often dismayed to see how little they have engaged with their audience and, mystifyingly, how often they turned to the screen where nothing had changed or there was very little to see. Why do they do this? It is not that the presenter is taking anything from the slides; rather, they are averting their gaze from the audience. They become almost like holograms: talking but not listening, present but not really there at all. This lack of engagement with the audience is very common and very damaging.

The Reason

There is a lot of talk about body language but nearly all of it – hand gestures, facial expressions, vocal intonation – takes care of itself. You don't have to remind your hands to move, you don't have to tell your voice to change pitch with a question; these things happen naturally. But the one element of body language that can cease when you are making a presentation is eye contact.

This goes to the core of what happens to people when they are under pressure. In a presentation, you have many things on your mind – the laptop, the projector, your time limit, your guide notes, the wobble you're sure everyone can hear in your voice – and the last thing you want to distract yourself with is the audience. They're likely to put you off so there is a tendency to shut them out. This is not really a fear response so much as a cognitive one. Your brain is overloaded and you need time to think, so you look away. You can observe this in people at quizzes or in exams. As they trawl their memories for answers they're sure they know, they close their eyes and cover their ears to concentrate more fully.

When people are concentrating, as in the picture on the right, they avert their eyes. This can be a problem for stressed presenters who have so much on their minds that they end up shutting the audience out.

You'll see the same thing in someone who is flustered. 'Where are my keys? What time is it? Where did I leave my bag?' In this state of mind they won't engage with the people around them and they won't make eye contact. The problem, though, is that a lack of eye contact damages a communication more than any other behaviour. Not only does it affect the way the audience feels but it robs the presenter of key metering behaviours that enable them to gauge and adapt to how the presentation is going.

As well as the stress of presenting, there is probably another reason why people don't engage with the audience as they would in a conversation: we tend to think of a presentation as a performance. Presentations are given in a conference room to a hushed audience often with the lights dimmed. Latecomers tiptoe to their seats with excruciating delicacy and questions are kept to the end. And when it's over, a strange thing happens: there is a polite round of applause.

This is bizarre when you think about it.

You wouldn't get applause for submitting a report on time or for serving someone in a shop. But due to its theatrical connotations, applause is the norm after a presentation, so much so that it would seem weird if one were to end in silence. This further removes the presenter from the audience and discourages eye contact, which is not good.

The Solution

There is a very easy fix and I know this because I had to fix it myself. I always liked giving presentations – I got nervous but I was fascinated by the challenge of trying to make complex ideas simple – but unbeknown to me, I was doing something wrong. And I'm thankful to the boss who pointed this out because the advice your elders and betters give you about presentations, as we will see in chapter 7, often does more harm than good. But what this guy said was spot on: 'The presentation was good, Barry, but you're not looking at the people in the room. You're in your own little world up there.'

We start making eye contact at a very early age and it continues to be the most potent element of communication throughout our lives. Did you turn your head to look at the baby in the picture above? Making eye contact is such a strong instinct that you do it automatically.

My boss was right and my behaviour was surprisingly easy to change. I kept hearing his voice in my head reminding me to look up and, in doing so, my awareness of the audience grew. It was like when your mother would say to you, 'Look at the lady when you're thanking her,' and it starts to become a habit. But this habit turned out to be more powerful than I imagined. To understand why, we need to look more closely at how eye contact works in conversations.

Listening with Your Eyes

The image below shows stills from a video-recording of a woman conversing with two other people. In the first image she is looking down, thinking as she speaks, and in the second she is glancing momentarily at one of the people in the group. This is normal; we don't stare constantly when we're talking but instead make intermittent eye checks, particularly at the end of small chunks of thought.

Contrast this, however, with a portion of the conversation where the woman is listening, shown in the second pair of images below. As she listens to the person opposite – whose hands you can just see on the right of the second frame – her stare is unbroken. This is an important point: people make more eye contact when they're listening than they do when speaking. It makes sense when you think about it; the listener has to read the speaker's lip movements, hand gestures, facial expressions and emotions, so they need to keep their eyes trained on the communicator. And this is an important lesson for presenters because making good eye contact shows that you are listening to your audience.

It may sound a odd to think of the presenter 'listening' to the audience, as he or she is doing most of the talking, if not all of it. However, making good eye contact shows that you are alert to the responses of the people in front of you and open to questions. This has a huge impact on the atmosphere in the room, making the audience feel – even if most don't ask a question – that they could do so. With this, you bring yourself onto the level of the listeners in a very intimate way. Without it, you are just a hologram.

Checking, Not Staring

The way I think of eye contact revolves around 'asking questions' not stressing points. By looking at the audience you are checking with them – 'Are you with me?' 'Does that make sense?' 'Any questions?' – but without saying these things out loud.

Imagine that each point you make is a handout and by moving your eyes around the room you are saying to people: 'Did you get one?' 'Did you?' 'And you?' We do exactly the same thing in a conversation where it helps that you can hear the listener say things like, 'Yes' 'Um' and 'I see'. They're not saying, 'I agree with you,' but rather, 'I understand that.' The listener is guiding the speaker and the audience in your presentation will be doing exactly the same thing, albeit silently.

This eye contact doesn't just help the audience, it helps the presenter, too. The figure above shows five stills from consecutive portions of another conversation. The images are about ten seconds apart. The speaker – the man with the beard – is explaining something to two listeners with the help of photographs on his phone. As he does this, his gaze alternates between the phone in his hand and the audience. What is interesting is that he lifts his eyes to check for understanding – as seen in frames 3 and 5 – at the end of each small chunk of thought, effectively the end of a long sentence.

The other thing that happens when he makes these eye fixes is that he stops speaking, just momentarily. And one further thing occurs; the listeners mumble their 'um's and 'I see's at exactly these points, and even ask a question after the last one. The whole thing is synchronised and yet completely subconscious, and it has the effect of slowing the speaker down, leading him to stress his points and involve the audience all at the same time. Eye contact in a presentation works in exactly the same way!

There is one last point on this which isn't an issue in conversations but which can be in a presentation. If you have a large audience, you cannot make eye contact with everyone, so what do you do? The key thing is to pick out individuals in every corner of the room. Do this no matter how awkwardly shaped or dimly lit the room is, and it will create a powerful inclusive effect. Each person in the audience, although the presenter may not have looked directly at them, will have seen the speaker engage with the person next to them, or in the row just in front, or the one just behind; so looking within given 'areas' will envelope a number of people. This makes that presenter seem inclusive, engaged and alert, and it makes an enormous difference.

The montage of images in the above figure demonstrates this process at work. Usually the presenter will – and should be – standing up, but this excerpt comes from a discussion at the end of a longer workshop, and by sitting down, the presenter was creating a more democratic, inclusive feel to encourage participation. The upper image gives you the context of his position in the room and you can see how spread out the audience is. And yet, as the lower series of images shows, the speaker makes sure to include people from all corners of the space around him, even, in the third frame, craning his neck to look at the woman sitting behind. Experienced speakers do this naturally but it is an easy habit to learn, and it is also a very important and potent one.

Better Engagement

Of course there is another way you can look like you are having a conversation with the audience: *just have one.*

Instead of looking like you are asking questions with your eyes, why not actually ask questions? As we shall see in chapter 5, interactivity is a presentation's greatest strength. You cannot interact, in real-time, with a book, a website or an email, and yet most presentations are stupidly non-interactive. Someone is asked to give a 20-minute presentation and they speak for 25 of these 20 minutes, not even leaving time for questions at the end. You don't have to wait till the end; you can engage the audience during the presentation. Ask them questions, get them to ask you questions, seek a show of hands, take breaks, go slow. Anything that gives the audience a chance to get involved is a good thing. And the first step in encouraging this interactive spirit is making frequent eye contact.

CHAPTER 3

Fear – Nerves Are Good, Caution Kills

The Problem

There is no point avoiding this issue any longer. The biggest problem most of us have when giving a presentation is nerves, and for some people this is crippling. But like so many topics in this book, our understanding of the issue is all wrong.

If nerves present such a big problem then overcoming nerves would seem like a great solution. Except it solves nothing.

Nerves are *your* problem, not the audience's. The audience don't care a damn about your nerves. They have problems of their own; they need to sit through a long presentation and keep their eyes open for starters. And a fearful presenter can make their problems a great deal worse but not in the way that you might think.

The Reason

To understand this issue, I need to distinguish between two types of fear, which from now on I will refer to as 'nerves' and 'caution'. Nerves strike on the day of a presentation, usually reaching a peak just before you start to speak, and they have obvious symptoms such as racing heart, shortness of breath, swirling stomach, sweaty palms, dry mouth and even shivering. Not everyone experiences nerves in their severest form but nearly everyone gets them to some degree. They key thing about nerves, though, is that they usually help. They do more good than harm, they only feel like they do harm. So don't worry about nerves, they won't impair your presentation.

Nerves are a good thing, they give you
energy and get you ready.

What about 'caution'? Caution strikes, not on the day of the presentation, but in the weeks leading up to it. Caution affects you when you are preparing your material but unlike nerves, it is symptomless. And unlike nerves, caution does untold damage.

I could paraphrase the caution mindset as follows: 'Don't do anything unusual; people won't like it.'

Let me give you an example. I was at the half-day launch of a large programme of EU-funded research at the National Convention Centre in Dublin a few years back, and the event opened with a series of quick-fire presentations. There were five high-profile speakers on the bill including a government minister and an Irish MEP, and the 2000-seater auditorium is a top of the range facility with semi-reclining seats, excellent acoustics and a knock-out high definition screen. I was looking forward to a good show! But I certainly didn't get one. So what was wrong? Well, for starters, the presentations were all speeches.

The problem with speeches is that they are pre-written. There is no spontaneity and no real-time connection with the audience. The speaker decides in advance what he or she is going to say and then reads it out, word for word. Boring! Not only is the cadence of a speech unlike that of natural conversation and therefore harder on the ear, but the fact that the speaker – or 'reader' – is going to plod through his or her material regardless of anything the audience does or says, is very disconcerting. For the two politicians who were presenting there was the excuse that everything they say would go 'on the record', and a certain amount of pre-planning was prudent, but they could have bookended the written portion of their speeches with something a little more alive and personable; for the other three speakers there was no such excuse.

Speeches are actually colossally overrated. Of course there have been a few good ones – '*Ich bin ein Berliner*,' and all that – but these occur infrequently, accompany momentous events in history, and are given by great orators. The best ones get replayed and mesmerise people into thinking they are a nice idea but rarely can they compete with a knowledgeable person just talking. Writing everything down in advance is a classic example of caution – avoid mistakes at all costs – and there were several others at this event.

Speeches and presentations are very different. Few people in the world can deliver a good pre-written speech; anyone can give a good presentation.

All of the presentations ran over time, most enormously so: 15 minutes instead of the allotted five. There were no stories, no images, no interesting data graphics, no videos, no demonstrations, no interaction with the audience, and next to no humour or emotion. The presentations had none of the things that actually make a presentation worth listening to. You may think I'm being harsh and argue that, for example, there is no time for interaction in a five-minute presentation, or that it is not practical to have a live demonstration, or that it is inappropriate to tell a story. But as we shall see later in this book, you can do all of these things, very easily, and you should. Caution prompted these speakers to give their presentations just like everybody else, and not in a good way.

The thing I found really interesting, though, was that the presenters at this event all had vast experience of public speaking. Ministers and MEP's, senior civil servants and college provosts; they'd done this kind of thing – if not always to such a large audience – hundreds of times before. They wouldn't suffer from nerves in the same way that most people reading this book would, and yet their presentations were lousy. So it wasn't nerves that was killing them, it was caution.

The Solution

I have two problems to solve here: how to overcome 'caution' and how to overcome 'nerves'. And it probably won't surprise you that I'm going to tackle the more serious problem first.

1. Overcoming Caution

For the Technical Communication course I teach at University College Dublin, students give really interesting presentations on the most diverse topics: fracking, bitcoin, bioprinting, the sounds drugs make in the brain, the rules of American football, statistical regression, 3D printing, space debris, social capital, scientology, bluetooth, Zipf's law and transhumanism, among others. And the communication approaches vary hugely. There has been a planetarium-like depiction of solar flares with lights dimmed and astral animations playing on-screen. There has been a subversion of the classic statistics coin-tossing experiments where coins were bent in vice-grips. An airbag was detonated in a presentation on automotive safety, a buzzer-containing cushion was thrown around the room in a presentation on the Doppler effect, and a ping-pong ball was levitated on a hair dryer to explain the Bernoulli effect and show how airplanes fly. Videos have been shot, edited, captioned and even scored, images have been cropped, shopped, zoomed and faded out. Examples have been cited and stories have been told. Lots of stories. And when I see all of this, I think to myself: *this is great, this course works.*

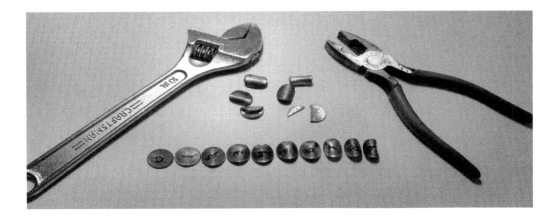

A novel, hands-on approach to teaching Bayesian statistics.

So when I was invited to a series of presentations that a group of statistics students, who had done my course, were giving to lecturers in their own school, I was keen to see this creativity in action. But things didn't quite go as I expected.

Instead of provocative images, demonstrations and stories, I saw quite a few bullet points and equations. This wasn't the case for all of the presentations but it was the case in more of the presentations than I was prepared for. Some of the students, despite all my entreaties to the contrary, were, when the pressure came on, playing it safe. Just like the presentations in the conference centre, higher stakes prompted an attack of caution.

I thought long and hard about why this had been and it struck me that many of these presentations had been aimed too squarely at the student's supervisors and not at a more general real-life audience. Which brings up a very interesting point about having you boss in the audience.

If you have prepared a presentation at work, you will probably wish to do a dry-run and get some feedback, and the person who will most likely give you this feedback is your boss.

However, your boss is often – not always but very often – the worst person to give you such feedback. Why? Because your boss knows what you are talking about, inside-out, and will not hear it the same way that your target audience will. The cautious statistics presentations definitely suffered from this and I have seen the same thing in companies many times. Your well-meaning boss doesn't want you to make mistakes, but the thing about communication is that the harder you try not to put a foot wrong, the surer you become of getting everything wrong. You have to take a few risks; you have to find novel ways to reach your audience.

Your boss will often be the worst person to give you feedback on your presentation.

Caution, however, prevents people from taking risks. Presenters defend dull material on the grounds that more interesting content would be gimmicky or inappropriate. But what's 'appropriate' about boring your audience? And why would it be 'gimmicky' to include, say, practical demonstrations, pictures or real-world examples that help people to understand what the hell you are talking about? Certainly everything has to be relevant and you should never include spicy content just to liven things up. But people respond to the same communication tools and always will: stories, real-life examples, demonstrations, analogies, videos, being listened to – i.e. interaction – and infectious enthusiasm. A presentation is a creative thing; one size definitely does not fit all. There are hundreds of ways you can explain any single idea and it is lazy and ineffective to take the first cautious approach that comes into your head. You have to generate multiple solutions and select the best ones. This is the simple creativity I am talking about and this will cure you of the malaise of caution.

So my practical guide to eliminating the ill-effects of cautions is as follow:

- Get feedback from someone you trust, ideally *not* your boss.
- Be creative. Generate many ideas. Pick the best ones.
- If you think something might be a bit dull, it almost certainly will be. Trust your instincts. Make your presentation as interesting as possible and hope that your audience find it interesting as well.
- Take a few risks.

2. Overcoming Nerves

I have played down the problem of nerves for two reasons. Firstly, because it's not a problem that will damage your presentation and therefore should not really concern you. And, secondly, because I don't really have a solution.

You will probably always be a bit nervous before a presentation but that's no bad thing. Nerves give you energy and lead you to ask important questions about what you're doing; they shake you up. The only downside to nerves is the tendency to speak too quickly. However, fewer people do this than you might expect. On courses, I often ask, 'Who thought they spoke too fast when making their presentation?' and generally more than half the group will raise a hand, even though sometimes no one has. The misperception results from a speedy brain not a speedy mouth. The presenter cannot actually remember what he or she has just said, but, crucially, the audience can.

You can see the benefit of nerves when you observe someone who doesn't suffer from them. I attended a course on third-level teaching, once, and the following was the opening line from one of the keynote speakers. 'I'm sorry,' he said, 'but I didn't know I had to give this talk until ten minutes ago.' Then he corrected himself. 'Or rather, I forgot that I'd agreed to give this talk until ten minutes ago,' and then he spoke for half-an-hour. The speaker was a college professor and he wasn't at all flustered or hurried as he droned his way through thirty minutes of ill-prepared material, which I ascribe to not being nervous enough. The absence of nerves leads to complacency, even arrogance, which is absolutely not a good thing. Nerves, by contrast, make you alert.

People only take an interest in what you are saying if you look like you care, as with the speaker above. Presenters who don't get nervous often lack this urgency.

The word I find myself using more and more in relation to presentations is: *urgency*. And it's not just urgency in delivery but urgency in preparation. If a slide is not clear, don't apologise for it, change it so that it is clear. If a video will show something better than a picture, find one on YouTube or shoot one yourself, or ask someone else to shoot one for you. Have the urgency to seek better ways to communicate and use your nerves to energise you to do so.

Self-Obsessed Presenters

The obsession with nerves is a classic presentation failing. People are so obsessed with how they are feeling that they lose sight of the more important point: how are the audience feeling? Are they getting anything out of this? Have you interested them? Have you taught them anything? Have you made them happy? Although you may be a jangling mess on the inside, most nerves are invisible from the outside. In any case, the audience doesn't really care that you didn't sleep last night or skipped breakfast this morning; why should they? They are giving up their time to listen to you and you should worry more about their needs than your nerves.

There is a soap opera going on in everyone's head but you just don't see it. You may feel like a quivering, yammering mess on the inside but the audience won't notice.

There are several suggested methods for tackling nerves directly but I have never found any to be much use. Many people say that deep breathing helps, so that might be worth a try. But the best medicine of all is rigorous preparation. Take the time to put together really good material and then thin it down to the bare essentials. On the day, get to the venue early and make sure everything is right. Check the slideshow, play the videos, try out the whiteboard pens, tap the microphone, find the power sockets, find a table for your notes, get yourself a glass of water, stay calm, be ready. Have backups prepared and do plenty of dry-runs. If you are nervous about things going wrong, do as much as you can to make sure they go right. With experience, your nerves will diminish and with every presentation your confidence will grow.

I remember the first time I gave a lecture… I was truly rattled. I was going before 200 students teaching them one of their toughest subjects. The lecture was scheduled for quarter-past-eleven so I got into the college well before nine and went to the canteen to look over my notes. Then I did something I had never done before or since: I spilled an entire cup of coffee into my lap.

Fortunately I was psyched up enough – and the coffee had cooled enough – that I didn't experience any pain or permanent scarring. But I did have a stupid looking coffee-stain on my unfortunately light-coloured trousers. So I found a bathroom where I soaped and watered them furiously before wearing them dry over the next two hours. The lecture went fine and 17 years on I still give lectures but, as you can imagine, they don't affect me quite the same way. I don't sleep poorly or fumble hot drinks over myself but I do find, maybe 20 minutes before the lecture begins, that I'm busy checking things over and have become aware, minute by minute, what time it is. With experience, your fear-response will kick in less severely – and closer in time to the presentation – but it will kick in nonetheless. And it's no bad thing that it does.

One thing that does help me reduce nerves is visiting the venue in advance. I'm not sure why this works, perhaps because it reduces the biggest fear of all: fear of the unknown. By being in the actual room and doing a few checks with the laptop and projector, I don't feel nearly as edgy about the upcoming event. Now I can picture the presentation in my head.

If it is not possible to visit the venue, I will contact the event organiser and ask them for an image or description of the room, and as much information as possible about the audience and what they might be looking for. Then, on the day, I will get there as early as I can to set up, check things over and meet people as they arrive. And I'm amazed how often other presenters turn up just minutes before kick-off to find there is no adaptor for their Mac, insufficient bandwidth to stream their YouTube clips, or no pens to write with or flip-chart to write upon. Often this is followed by a pointed look at the organiser as if to say, 'You've let me down.' But as I always say: it may not be your fault but it is definitely your problem. If you're interested in controlling nerves, don't invite a horror-show like this on yourself.

So my practical guide to eliminating nerves is quite simple:

- Prepare thoroughly, practice, seek opportunities to present.
- Get to the venue early and talk to the audience beforehand.
- Breathe deeply and slowly, and drink plenty of water.
- Allow nerves to energise you and know that they do more good than harm.

Then enjoy the ride.

CHAPTER 4

Running Out of Time – The Art of Zooming

The Problem

Despite the fact that most people don't like giving presentations, the majority of them run over time. Which is odd. If giving a presentation is so unpleasant – like swimming in the sea in February – you'd imagine that a nervous speaker would be keen to get it over with. But presenters always seem to have too much to say, which leads to overrunning presentations or the presenter speaking so fast that nobody understands a word they say.

The Reason

The problem is characterised by a refrain I often hear from presenters: 'It's so hard to shrink everything down to just ten minutes,' or 'This topic is too complex to explain in such a short presentation.' This, however, frames the presentation as a compression of a large quantity of information which is not how it should be seen. It should actually be viewed as an *expansion*, not a *compression*, which is something people easily get in conversations.

Imagine you met someone at a party and they asked you what you do for a living. How would you reply? Think about this for a second. I'm guessing your response would be along the lines of: 'I'm an engineer,' or, 'I'm a school teacher,' or 'I'm a professional tennis player.' In other words, it will only take you one or two seconds to answer the question. That could be a 30 year career summarised in two seconds.

Of course, the person you say this to may ask for more. 'Oh, you're a teacher; my wife's a teacher. Are you primary school or secondary school?' Or they may take the conversation in a different direction entirely. The point is you dip into a topic, deeper and deeper, based on the perceived interest of the listener. You won't just launch into a 10- or 20-minute account of your entire career. So why are we compelled to do this in a presentation?

FAQ

One thing I always say to presenters is: pay close attention to the questions people ask at the end of your presentation as this often indicates important things you left out. For example, people are often reluctant to tell stories in presentations – something we'll look at in chapter 8 – but the audience will seek them afterwards. 'Have you used one of these devices yourself?' 'Did you try the recipe?' 'How did you get into this stuff?' So it's a good idea to think of a presentation like the FAQs – 'frequently asked questions' – you see on websites. Think: what will they most want to know? If I tell them that, what might they ask next? It's even a good idea to include these as signposting rhetorical questions in the talk. 'Now, having looked at the theory, how do we put this into practice?' But there is another good reason to see the presentation as answers to a series of questions: it forces you to consider the audience's problems, not your own.

Think of the questions the audience might ask. This will put you
in the right frame of mind for planning your content.

Consider the following true story. Recently, a Chinese student came to me looking for the person in charge of overseas registration. I'm seated just inside the door in an open-plan office and I often end up fielding queries of this sort. But this guy had come to totally the wrong place, so I told him where to go – down one flight of stairs, across the hallway and through the double-doors – and he thanked me and went on his way. That's the story.

So what? Well, let's flip the scenario around. Imagine I was asked to give a presentation on my work at University College Dublin. That's 19 years, so I should have quite a lot to say. How long do I have for this presentation? Let's say it's 10 minutes. So, by a simple calculation, that's around two years per minute, or just under a fortnight per second. But of course that's not the way I would approach it. Like any story, I can summarise and zoom and pick out the most interesting bits. But there have been a lot of changes to courses and educational methods on those years, as well as to my own role, so I still might find it hard to know where to start. And yet, when that Chinese student asked me where the overseas office was, out of all my knowledge and experience of UCD, I pulled out just one piece of information and answered his question in ten seconds flat.

This is how you should think of a presentation, as *the answer to a question*. And the more specific you make that question the better. What most people do is *define a presentation in terms of what they know, not what the audience needs to hear*. Then they broadcast 20 minutes of what they know and leave the audience to take something from this, like browsers at a jumble sale. But functional conversations don't work like this and a real-world example may help to explain why.

Consider a doctor-patient consultation. Although this is a one-to-one communication, not one-to-many, in every other respect it is a perfect exemplar for a presentation. There is an expert who knows stuff – lots of stuff – and there is an audience who needs to hear some of that stuff to solve a problem. It is not just interesting facts and insights, it is a means to an end. And the doctor doesn't give the patient a PowerPoint presentation on viral infections – different types, most common symptoms, treatments, expected outcomes, etc. – but rather gives the audience just enough information to make him- or herself well.

Interestingly, a doctor-patient consultation shares many other features with a good presentation. It is short (annoyingly so, sometimes), interactive (the patient is encouraged to ask questions), personal (the body language and emotional demeanour of the doctor are important), it may have stories, images and demonstrations (demonstrations always featured in my all-too frequent visits to the physiotherapist when I was playing football), and it is highly engaging. You are unlikely to be bored listening to a doctor tell you what's wrong with you. And like a doctor, when you are preparing a presentation, you need to think about the needs of the audience, and nothing more. What's wrong and how can you make it right? Then you can draw on your knowledge but only to the extent that it solves their problem.

A doctor-patient consultation, apart from being a one-to-one, rather than a one-to-many communication, has all the features of a good presentation.

The Solution

To address this, I want to explain a concept I call the 'communication chain'. This outlines where a presentation fits into a wider sequence of communication steps and will help you to figure out what should go into a presentation and, crucially, what should be left out.

Imagine you get an email at work and in the subject line it refers to a lunchtime presentation which you think might be interesting. So you open and read the email, and decide to pencil the date into you diary. Let's say the talk is about time management and you go along and it turns out to be really good. What happens next? Well, quite likely you'll approach the speaker afterwards and ask a few questions, and you might even arrange a follow-on meeting. What happens after that? You're still enthused so you ask the presenter if he or she has a website or if there are any books they would recommend. So you read further into the topic and eventually change the way the way you work by implementing some of the ideas you've learnt. All of this based on one presentation? Well, not quite.

The key thing to observe here is that the presentation sits within a chain of other communications and the timescale of each expands as you move along the chain. The title of the talk grabbed you in a few seconds. The description – in that first email – was read in a minute. The talk lasted for 20 minutes. The follow-on meeting for half-an-hour. The website took a few hours to browse. The book took two weeks to read. Implementing the ideas may continue to happen over the next few years. At any stage, you might decide to stop and go no further, but if you are interested you feel your way along this chain, getting deeper and deeper into the topic with increasing investments of time. The point to note is that the presentation, transient and short as a presentation necessarily is, always comes early in this chain.

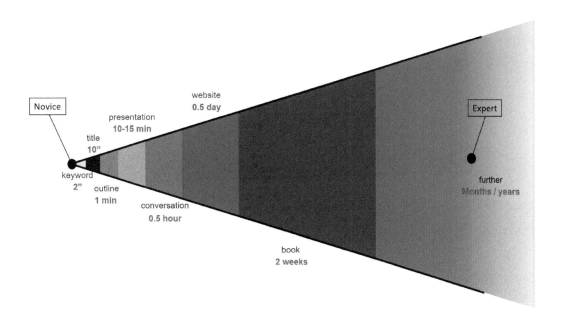

A presentation always comes early in the 'communication chain'. Your job as a presenter is not to tell the audience everything you know in 15 minutes but simply to move them to the next stage in this chain.

Indeed, most communications follow a chain like this. Consider a television programme. The title – *Wife Swap, Masterchef, Match of the Day* – grabs your attention at a glance. Then a sentence in the TV schedules will tell you what episode it is, or if it is a repeat. Then a paragraph will describe what the programme is about. You watch the programme… but what happens after? Broadcasters have long seen the value in communications that happen before the programme airs – catchy titles, trailers, advertisements – but in the digital age, they are now increasingly thinking about what happens afterwards. You are invariably invited to visit the programme's website or 'press the red button' on your remote control to find out more. But just like the presentation example, the timescales extend as you move along the chain. And just like the chain for a presentation, these links are all very different in nature.

Which points us to the mistake that many presenters make. They try to cram 10 years of experience into 10 minutes of presentation, but it doesn't go. And the formatting and structure of the presentation are all wrong. There are spidery graphs and wads of text that might sit well in a detailed follow-on report but not in a live presentation. The links in the communication chain are squashed together and morphed into one form when each should be distinct and specialised. And you can often spot this problem in the very first link in the chain: *the title*! Consider this one:

'Fitting Parametric Multivariate Copula Survival Models'

Would you go to this presentation? I didn't. And you might think I'm being glib, rubbishing the boffin's techno-babble titles, but the point is, I *was* the target audience for this presentation. It was advertised in the university newsletter as an invitation to a public talk. So it was aimed at me as much as anyone else. But surely no one but a specialist could engage with such a title. What about this one?

'Topology Optimization Using Barycentric Discretization: Theory and Applications'

Any takers? This was in an email for another public lecture, albeit within the faculty where I work. I still didn't understand a word of it, though. One more:

'Experimental Study of the Effect of Inlet Valve Generated Turbulence on the Rate of Combustion in a 2.5 Litre Naturally Aspirated Direct Injection Diesel Engine'

This one I do understand because it is the title of the presentation I gave on my own Masters in 1996. It's a classic example of *not* understanding the communication chain in that I have used the title of my thesis as the title of my presentation.

What I was failing to grasp at the time was that the thesis and the presentation were two totally different things, two widely separated parts of the communication chain. The presentation was to staff and students over coffee on a Tuesday afternoon. None of them really gave a damn about 'inlet valve-generated turbulence' and the talk was only 20 minutes long, so how could I possibly break down all of the concepts announced in the title alone? The thesis, on the other hand, was a 200 page document which told the story of a complex and demoralizingly catastrophe-strewn 30 months of work, so there was no reason for the two communications to share the same name. They were as different as a CD and a painting.

So, from this idea of the communication chain, I would urge you to think about two things when planning your next presentation. First, the aim is not to make your audience experts by the end of your talk, the aim is simply to move them to the next step in the chain. Second, think about what this next step is – and subsequent steps – and plan material for these, as well. These two points combined will allow you to thin down and simplify your presentation content enormously.

Setting an Aim

The position a presentation takes in the communication chain explains, I think, why many presenters don't take them seriously. If you give a good presentation, you might provoke a discussion or entice people to your website or be invited to give a follow-on presentation at a higher level. Rarely will a short presentation be rewarded with instant riches or a huge contract. However, a bad one will break the communication chain and deny you this reward at a later stage. It's impossible, though, for you to see how things *might* have turned out if you'd given a better presentation, so people undervalue the power of that presentation to move their audience forward. But power it has. You could send 1,000 emails to 1,000 would-be clients, but none will give you the same traction as three minutes face-to-face, telling your audience what you know and why they should care.

The key thing is to set a realistic aim. Ask yourself: what will the audience do that they wouldn't or couldn't do before listening to me? This sounds like a tall order for a short presentation but the sentence has two key words: 'audience' and 'do'. In other words, your aim should not be: 'I will talk about…' or 'I will cover…' but rather, 'The audience will…'

Also, the outcome for the audience should be active, not passive. Your aim should not be: 'The audience will hear about…' or, 'The audience will learn…' but rather, 'This presentation will enable the audience to…' or, 'At the end of my talk, the audience will…' The outcome might be to ask questions, have a discussion, take a flyer or make a decision with a show of hands, but the more you try to imagine follow-on actions, the more focused your choice of content will be.

A presentation should be like a cookery programme. It does not just convey information but instead helps the audience do something tangible with that information.

Even if the talk is a stand-alone interest-piece, and not part of any grand plan on your part, you should still try to make the take-away points as portable as possible. So instead of calling a presentation, say, 'The basics of good nutrition,' you might have, 'Three healthy recipes for busy people'. Or instead of, 'Occupational Health and Fitness,' you might have, 'Exercises you can do at your desk.' These more focused presentations with tangible outcomes will still contain many of the same facts and ideas, but the presentation will have an arrow-like quality and go somewhere. It will also have a catchier title.

It is important to note, however, that my retitling of presentations above is not just a process of rebranding or reordering your material, but of selecting the right material in the first place. You may be a dietician with decades of experience but you don't have time to explain flavonoids and free radicals; you need to deliver something useful to the audience – 'three healthy recipes for busy people' – as quickly as possible. This will still necessitate some background theory, as people won't buy into your recommendations if they don't see a body of knowledge behind them, but the theory is incidental, not central, and the presentation as a result is clearer. And shorter.

One of the most famous examples of this thinking came from Apple founder, Steve Jobs, on the release of the iPod. I was never a Steve Jobs acolyte and I have very little interest in gadgets and the 'next big thing', but having grown up with Walkmans and then moved on to a Discman that was so jumpy I had to carry it around like a tray of cocktails, I could see that the iPod, with its hundred-CD capacity, was a massive leap forward. I could also see what an amazing feat of electronics, ergonomics and elegance it was. And yet, when Steve Jobs presented this technical wonder to the world, he didn't talk about the product's phenomenal technical specs or how roundly it trounced the opposition, he simply said, 'A thousand songs in your pocket'. That's what it did for the customer, so that's all they needed to hear.

'A thousand songs in your pocket.' Steve Jobs' immortal tagline didn't describe any of the iPod's ground-breaking technology or design, but simply told the audience what it would do for them. Your presentation should do the same for your audience. Quickly.

I made a set of talking-heads videos for my online course a few years ago, and one of the contributors vocalised this idea very succinctly. John O'Sullivan works for Eirgrid, who manage the electricity network in Ireland, and he frequently makes presentations to a range of different audiences: managers, policy makers, the public and his own team. Jonno vocalised how he feels when he is in the audience at a presentation: 'For me, a presentation is: tell me why this is important to me. Quickly, please.'

This highlights a very important point. Your audience will probably seem calm, polite and patient, even a little docile. But that doesn't mean they are calm and patient on the inside. On the inside they will be drumming their fingers and shifting in their seats. On the inside they will l be asking: *Why the hell are you telling me this?* And this is not selfishness or cynicism, it's cognitive efficiency. Faced with the information that bombards us every waking second of our lives, we constantly make assessments of what we need to consider and remember, and what we can discard. So you need to help the audience to do this by organising your material around *their* needs and *their* knowledge, not your own. Don't waste their time.

The Red Button

When you have figured out what goes into your presentation, it is easy to work out what should come afterwards. For example, I use my first book as notes – I give a physical copy to each participant – on courses that I give, which leaves me free to focus on discussions, group exercises and presentation feedback on the day. What I'm hoping is that, having done the course, attendees may *want* to read the book. If, however, I went to a local shopping mall and handed copies of my book out to passers-by, some may take one out of politeness, but I can't imagine any would read it. In many ways, the presentation can be seen as a justification of follow-on material, a pitch for it. In the presentation, you are trying to create enough curiosity so that the audience will proceed along the communication chain to the next step.

I use my first book as course-notes. This, I hope, will become the next step in the communication chain for my audience, where they can go to find out more.

One other point about the communication chain is that you shouldn't hide it from the audience. It's not a subliminal message, you want them to know what comes next. So say things at the start like, 'Don't worry about taking notes, all the theory and all the links are included in the document I've given you.' Or, 'At the end of this presentation, I would like to take a vote on what people think we should do.' Or, simply, 'Ask me a question any time.' Let them know what you want them to do.

My brother-in-law, Bob, who was operations director at Hovis, occasionally gives talks at management conferences. He realises, in a large auditorium, that many people will be nervous about asking questions or will not have time to do so. He also realises that people might be shy about approaching him after the talk. So he says, 'I may look quite serious, and you may be wary about approaching me after, but I will be here all day long, and the conversations I have with people throughout the day are as much a part of the training session as this presentation is. So feel free to come and talk to me or just contact me later at the following email address.' When I asked him about this he used an interesting word: '*abundant*'. 'You have to be abundant,' he told me. 'I'm happy to give and tell everything I know to everyone. Bad presenters aren't abundant. You get some people and you can tell that they're not prepared to do that. And people sense it, your integrity and your openness and your willingness to tell them everything.'

I would say one more thing about the Q&A session after a presentation. Earlier I suggested that the questions you are asked often reflect important things you left out. But if, as Bob terms it, you are an 'abundant' presenter, and your presentation is accessible and stimulating, people are likely to ask you anything. If I gave my Masters diesel engine presentation today, and made a really good job of it, I might easily get questions about the Volkswagen diesel emissions scandal, or diesel versus petrol cars, or global warming, or Formula One superchargers, or anything. If the audience is interested and trusts you, they will want to know what you think. And although it can discommode a presenter to be asked a question on something outside their scope, it is a far better when this happens than when you get no questions at all. The next chapter expands on this very point.

CHAPTER 5

Doing All the Talking – Interaction Is Key

The Problem

The ability to interact with your audience is probably the greatest strength of a presentation and yet it is an option that most presenters shun. In a breathless effort to 'cover' their material, they shut the audience out. This is more damaging than you think because if the audience is not talking, they may also not be understanding, or caring, or even listening.

The Reason

It may sound counterintuitive but the key to good presenting is not the ability to talk but the *ability to listen*. Maybe I should phrase this another way: presentations fail, not due to a poor grasp of the speaking process, but due to a poor grasp of the listening one.

Everyone can talk. Everyone. Easily. We can take the ideas in our heads and turn them into words in the time it takes us to think them. Speaking is something we have been practising since we were born. Babies typically don't say their first words until they are around one-year-old but the cause and effect of conversation – together with facial expressions, eye contact and body language that emphasise the spoken words – starts after just a few weeks.

When you learn how to speak fluently (which you do by the age of three) most people spend the rest of their lives – several hours a day, every day – practising. The average person puts in roughly 40,000 hours of speaking practice by the time they are 30-years-old, and in doing so, they perfect an extremely subtle and sophisticated palate of skills.

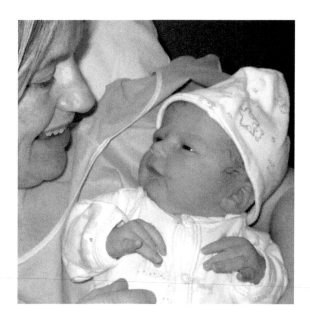

We start practicing our communication skills almost as soon as we are born.

For example, in a group conversation, you can tell from several feet away who someone is looking at even if they don't move their head. This is remarkable when you think about it. To switch gaze between two people several feet away involves pupil rotations of as little as 10 or 15 degrees. And if you consider that the pupil is only about half a centimetre wide, you are talking about displacements of just a fraction of a millimetre. Indeed, it has caused many arguments – 'I saw you looking at her' – between jealous couples.

Eye contact is just one of the subtleties of communication. We inflect, repeat and stress words to give them emphasis. The listener nods and utters a variety of sounds to pace and guide the speaker in the direction of clarity. We work automatically, in many-sided conversations, to figure out who speaks next through the subtle mechanism of 'turn-taking'. We prompt each other for examples – 'Oh, is that the same as..?' – to make ideas more tangible. We tell stories. We ask questions. We laugh. All of these things work seamlessly to make any ordinary person a sophisticated communicator.

My friends all make me laugh even though none are comedians. They all grip me with their stories even though none are actors or writers. If you are worried about giving your next presentation, you should remind yourself that you already know how to speak. Or rather, you're not going to learn anything new or better about speaking in the time it takes you to read this book. Your style is your own and it's actually highly accomplished already.

Listening, on the other hand, well, most people are not very good at. What you say doesn't matter as much as what the audience hears, and judging this is difficult. In my opinion, the inability of presenters to make good judgements about what the audience is hearing is the thing that damages oral presentations most.

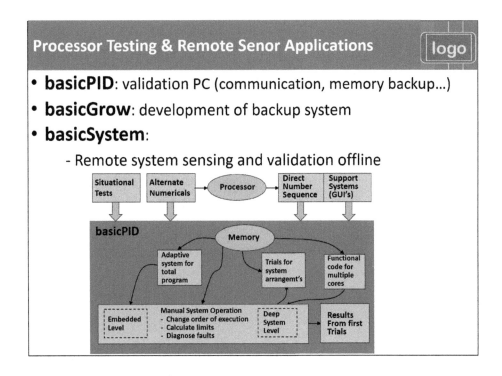

A not untypical presentation slide. It represents what the speaker wants the audience to know but it is not a good way of helping them to do so.

We looked at slides like the one above, previously. A slide like this captures what the presenter knows, not what the audience wants to hear. In this regard, it is indicative of poor insight into the listening process not the speaking one.

The presenter is focused on all of the things he or she wants to say and not mindful of what someone in the audience is actually hearing. Overloading slides is only one indication that the speaker doesn't understand the listening process. Putting text on screen and reading it out is another. People read through bullet points with great interest but the audience doesn't hear them with great interest. And there are many other daft practices that we look at in this book, which all point to the same thing: a poor grasp of listening.

The Un-Closed Feedback Loop

So why are presenters so poor at understanding what the audience is hearing? Well, it's obvious, really: no feedback. You have no way of knowing what the audience has actually heard. You cannot follow them around, months after your talk, and find out which things stuck with them, and which were forgotten. Even if you could, it would be difficult to link what they remembered to the tools you employed in your presentation. Did the picture make the penny drop? Was it the story? Should you have told a different story? Would they have remembered the point better or worse if you had?

If you open a restaurant and the food is lousy, you'll see it left on plates. People won't come. You'll lose money and have to close, or change the head-chef. But in a presentation there is nothing left on the plates. It is very difficult to judge from the blank, polite, passive faces you see before you, whether you have done a good job or not. As we saw in chapter 3, the person you are most likely to receive feedback from is your boss but often this is the last person you should be guided by. They probably understand your material too well and will not, therefore, represent a valid target audience. They will be bad listeners and no use to you. So how do you close this feedback loop?

Well, the way to do it is obvious and yet most people spurn the opportunity. The way to find out what they audience is hearing is to ask them. Interact with them. You cannot interact with an email or a book or a YouTube video, but a presentation is live. And you can derive so many benefits from this that it staggers me how seldom people avail themselves of this strength.

The Solution

Interaction enables you to meet the audience half-way and understand what they are failing to understand. But it actually does so much more than this. It transforms the feeling of a presentation and makes it much more engaging. However, there is one very important proviso: interaction is not something you can demand, it has to be willingly given. The audience has to want to interact or it doesn't count. You could just start picking on people in the audience at random but if this is intrusive or intimidating, it will do more harm than good. In the same way, you could walk up to a stranger on a crowded train and start talking to them but this is not a conversation. The person may answer but it only becomes meaningful when the ice is broken and they engage with you willingly.

Interaction is only meaningful when it is willing. In the same way, the words you exchange with a stranger only become a conversation when the other person talks back willingly.

The approaches detailed in this chapter are really ways of getting the audience to *want* to engage. Also, the ideal would be to have a room full of people sitting forward in their seats dying to ask you questions but there are other lighter forms of interaction you can encourage. So I have laid these interaction techniques out in order of 'full-blown-ness'. They range from 'full-strength interaction' to 'a hint of interaction' and you should be able to find something in this list that works for you. It is definitely important that you try.

Level 1 – Full Strength, Active

Let's start with the most direct form of interaction. Why not ask the audience a question instead of waiting for them to ask you one. Presenters are often afraid to do this in case they get no reply but there are several things you can do to prompt one.

What you have to remember is that any person who voices an opinion or asks a question is, just like you, speaking in front of the group. So they will be prey to the same nerves that affect you, only without the control and authority you, as the speaker, have. Coupled with this, most presentations are so one-sided, with the audience playing such a diminished role, that the expectation of having contributions from the floor is low. Consequently, people behave like passengers on a bus: waiting for their stop and generally keeping to themselves. So the first thing you have to do is create an atmosphere that encourages interaction, so that people are more likely to respond when you do ask them something.

At the start, tell the audience that you welcome their comments and questions. Most presentations are under-introduced. In a hurry to get started – and finished – the speaker takes off at a breath-taking pace without telling the audience where they are going or why.

Not only do you need to set a context at the start but you need to state the obvious stuff, like how long are you going to talk, what will happen after the presentation and, of course, that you welcome questions throughout. This may seem a little laboured but the audience is getting settled in their seats and used to the rhythm and pitch of your voice, so a content-less preamble is never a bad thing. It's like being at a party when you meet someone and in the flurry of friendly banter you realise you have forgotten – within seconds of hearing it – that person's name. People don't listen well at the start so you have to bring them in slowly. By doing this you not only get to say that you welcome interaction but you're also showing, through a calm, unhurried opening, that you mean it. You're setting a tone of, 'We're in no rush, here. Interrupt me whenever you want.'

If you want to be more proactive in getting the audience involved, there are many ways of doing this. Let me share an example from my own experience to show you what's possible, even with a large group. I used to give engineering lectures to a class of about 200 people. It was daunting at first but after a few weeks I got used to it and the class got used to me and I became fairly relaxed. Then, later in the term, I attended a course on third-level teaching and one of the topics under discussion was the age-old problem of student engagement. One very interesting approach was discussed. It involved asking students to cluster into small groups and spend a few minutes discussing a question you had put to them. Then you get them to submit a sheet with their ideas – anonymously – and review them afterwards. In the ensuing lecture, you feed the answers back to the class before tying things together with your own explanation.

Getting the audience to do something, anything at all, will enhance the effectiveness of your communication and make it more memorable.

The exercise was clever because the opinions of all students were canvassed and fed into the discussion in a way that would never happen by asking questions to the whole class. The mini-discussions were good for weaker students because they learnt from their peers, and helpful to the stronger students because of the educational benefits of having to explain your ideas to someone else. And the question posed was open-ended rather than one with a simple right or wrong answer, so that lines of creative thinking could be displayed even if students were on the wrong track. A great exercise, I thought to myself, and one I definitely planned to try out if I were teaching a smaller class.

But almost the instant I thought this, I realised I could just as easily do it with 200 people as I could with 20. And so I did. I ran the exercise in the very next lecture. I showed a short video clip of the Tacoma Narrows Bridge collapse – a suspension bridge dancing itself to destruction in the wind – which is a remarkable example of a concept called 'resonance'. I then set the class the task of writing down five yes/no questions they would ask me to find out what was happening. This allowed them to think creatively without butting against a single right or wrong answer. It also fuelled the small group discussions which they convened without batting an eyelid. I thought they might have been more reticent.

I collected the sheets and used them to platform a discussion in the next lecture, and it produced one of the most interesting classes of the year, for me as well as for the students. There were many interesting lines of enquiry regarding energy, design, materials, human behaviour and chance, several of which I would never have thought of myself. There were also funny questions like: 'Did a woman build the bridge?', 'Did a man build the bridge?', 'Was the bridge made of jelly? Is there any jelly left?', and even, 'What is the matrix?' So it was a highly successful exercise which I employed again and again, in different courses, in the ensuing years.

Not only does a task like this work in getting people active during a presentation but it breaks the ice and makes them more likely to respond to the questions you ask later on. And the great thing about interaction is that it doesn't just benefit the interactors. Some people are more active in their learning style and some are more reflective but, critically, an interactive environment benefits both. The reflectors may say less but they will enjoy what they hear more. Their 'reflection' will be more interesting because a conversation is easier to listen to than a speech. The pitch and rhythms of the voices are more natural, and the collaborative, informal atmosphere created is more cordial. So the interventions from the audience don't have to be continual and don't have to be from everyone to boost the interest of all.

One last point to make about asking the audience questions is to *take your time*. Silence can seem oppressive and weird to a nervous speaker, so no sooner do most presenters ask a question than they answer it themselves! Try to have a natural pause after asking a question in case there isn't an answer straight away. Take a sip of water or turn to the next page of your notes or change the slide. People are often keen to get involved but sometimes need a few seconds to find the nerve to do so. Without sweating contributions out of your audience, allow them some time to make the leap.

Level 2 – Full Strength, Passive

If you can't engage the audience, at least make it easy for them to engage you. There will nearly always be questions at the end of your presentation and presenters fear them but they are invariably the best bit. So don't dive for your seat as soon as you finish talking.

Tell the audience you welcome questions and spend a few seconds gathering up your stuff to give them a chance to ask you one. Also ask for questions as you go along. Often presenters say that they will 'take questions at the end' but this is really like saying, 'Shut up and listen.' And even though that's what people generally do, it doesn't create an inclusive atmosphere when you make it a rule.

The demeanour of the presenter can make a big difference to how the audience engage. It might not surprise you that this friendly group got asked many questions at the end of their presentation.

Even worse is when there is a group of presentations and the chair of the session requests that questions be held until the end of *all* the talks. An utterly ridiculous idea this. The best thing about a presentation is its live-ness and picking up on something a speaker said 40 minutes and three presentations ago is not 'live'. As a presenter, this kind of thing may be out of your hands but I would always try to work around it if I could. I'd seek a 'quick question or two' half way through the talk and reassure the room that you have built in enough time for these questions, as well as for a few more at the end.

Sometimes you won't get asked a question straight away but you can tell, by the positive atmosphere in the room, that you might get asked one if you wait. One thing you can do in this situation is ask yourself a question. This might sound daft but it's actually a nice technique and can be done subtly. You could say something like, 'Actually, one thing I'm often asked and I probably should have mentioned is...' Like the first dancer on the dance floor, one question usually prompts another and things pick up quickly.

When answering questions there are several dos and don'ts, and it would be remiss of me not to include the following quick-fire list on these.

Dealing with Questions

Be nice. Be very nice, in fact. As I said, the questioner might be more nervous than you. Some people ask stupid questions – although this may be because you didn't communicate your ideas clearly – some ask questions to show off, some even ask questions to catch you out, but you cannot afford to be hostile to anyone. Why? If you embarrass or berate one person, you are actually berating everyone in the room. It becomes a 'them-and-us' scenario and the audience are all on the same side. That's why presentations are so nerve-racking in the first place, because you have stepped outside of the group and taken up a different role relative to the others in the room. What you say to one will be felt by all... so tread carefully.

No matter how stupid, antagonistic or irrelevant the question is, try to be nice to the person who asked it.

If someone is really being disruptive, however – something that almost never happens but people worry about it endlessly – you can use that in your favour. The antagonistic questioner, if he or she keeps on, will no longer be serving the audience and that audience will disown them. I saw this, once, at a presentation where a group of undergraduate students had spent a summer studying Ireland's future energy needs and were presenting their conclusions to an invited audience at a showcase event. Because there was a government minister present, someone in the audience took the chance to raise a gripe on an unrelated matter. One of the students was chairing the session and, with remarkable confidence and calmness for someone so young, put the protestor firmly in his place. The reaction from the crowd was a round of applause. This protestor, with his personal agenda, was deflecting the audience from the presentation they had come to see. His need and their needs were no longer aligned so he could be cast out of the group. Remember, though, that this kind of put-down should be kept only as a last resort.

Repeat the question. People overdo this sometimes – 'Thank you for your really interesting question…' and so on – but there are reasons for repeating the question. First, many people in the room may not have heard it. A nervous questioner will not project his or her voice the same way the presenter will. Second, it gives you a chance to get the question clear in your head. Third, it buys you a bit of thinking time. In an intimate setting, it can be a bit laboured but it's generally a good idea.

Direct your answer to everyone. If your talk was relevant to everyone then your answers to questions should also be. Include everyone in the sweep of your eye and the positioning of your body. Start and end with the questioner; begin your answer focused on them, then bring your eyes back at the end, and even ask them if your answer made sense.

Don't over-answer. This can happen when a nervous presenter is so relieved to know the answer that they charge into their response like a dog let off his lead. Which prompts them to think of something else that they then talk about for minutes on end. If you do this with your first question, you won't get asked a second. Better to respond crisply and be ready for the next question like a tennis player returning a serve. This makes for a better dialogue and allows more people to take part.

Many people over-answer questions. If you do this with the first one,
you won't get a second. Better to give a concise answer and wait
for another, like a tennis-player returning a serve.

Don't under-answer. This is much less common but some experts will try to give the most concise and unadorned answers they can. 'No.' 'Yes.' 'Three.' 'It is.' At the heart of every question, however, is a need. Often, the question and the need will be aligned – 'Where are the toilets?' – but this is not always the case. I saw an example of this where the sales manager of a company was asking a senior technician questions but I could see the sales manager was confused and unhappy with the answers he was getting. However, he didn't have the expertise, background knowledge or vocabulary to vocalise his concern. The technician had answered his questions concisely but he wasn't addressing the need that lay behind them. It's a bit like when someone says, 'Is anyone going to eat that last slice of cake?' when what they actually mean is, 'Can I have it?' And it is yet another reason to repeat the question because in clarifying the question you clarify the need that motivated it, which can save a lot of time in the long run.

Don't answer if you don't know. Know what you are presenting and what you are not. If someone asks you a question outside this brief, don't be afraid to say you don't know. Why should you? People ask questions when they are interested and when they like you, as I said in the last chapter, and this is great but you have to be sensible in how you deal with such queries.

The simplest thing is to say you don't know but will endeavour to find out. I saw an excellent example of this at a conference where the keynote speaker was asked a question for which he had no answer. 'I don't know,' he replied, 'but there is a colleague of mine who probably does. So if you write the question on the back of a business card and give it to me afterwards, I'll look into it when I return to the office and email you a reply.' The presenter had dealt with the questioner's need, prevented the situation from upsetting his progress and been polite and urbane into the bargain.

Level 3 – Medium Strength, Pre-Planned

Con-men use the term 'shill', conjurors say 'plant'. Am I really suggesting that you set someone up in the audience to ask you a question? Well, yes and no. I'm not advocating a hoax, but it breaks the barriers between you and the audience when you bring someone from that audience into the discussion. The crucial point, though, is that you make sure that the person is OK with this, beforehand. Then it's simply a comment like, 'Grace, you had an experience like this, didn't you?' to set things in motion. You can even do it with an earlier speaker at the same event. This works very well because if the audience heard that person's presentation, then the example will be fresh in their minds.

I did this at a workshop in Brussels a few years ago. Although, when I say 'workshop', it was really just a procession of very one-sided presentations. However, one of the speakers broke out of this staid format, divided the room into small groups and did a 20-minute exercise to develop a hypothetical new product. It was a simple exercise but it produced some really interesting results. The other thing this speaker did – his name was Martin, by the way – was tell stories.

Before my session the following day, I approached Martin over coffee, complimented him on his workshop and said that I might mention it in my own talk if he didn't mind. Of course he didn't; why would he? Part of my own session was on story-telling as a communication tool and I referred to Martin's presentation from the previous day and asked him some questions. This kind of 'Martin, what do you think?' technique is very easy to implement and works really well because it turns your presentation into a conversation which transforms the atmosphere in the room. Another milder way of doing the same thing is to chat with people before the presentation and use these conversations in the presentation. You might simply say, 'I was discussing this with some people beforehand...' or 'This actually came up earlier…' Interestingly, you will notice that guests on radio programmes often do this when they say things like, 'I was just saying to your researcher...' We pick up on earlier conversations when engaging in subsequent ones. And although you don't want to put anyone on the spot, it can be a nice touch if you look in the direction of the person you are referring to (as if to say, 'Remember?'). It shows you are connected with the audience and even know some of them. It also shows that your presentation is tuned to that specific group and not something generic you roll out every time you speak.

Level 4 – Medium Strength, Deferred

We looked at this in the last chapter when we considered what comes after the presentation, that next step in the communication chain. Will you be around after the presentation to chat further? Until when? Would you be keen to hear people's experiences on certain topics? What topics? If you won't be sticking around, what is your email address or the URL of your website? Have you put these on the screen? Have you left them there long enough for people to write them down?

Level 5 – Mild Interaction

If you can't get people to be full-on 'interactive', at least get them to be 'active' in some way. They are more likely to remember what you say if they are doing something. There are many ways to get the audience active without leaving their seats or even saying anything. One is to ask for a show of hands. This is a good way to gauge opinion as the audience has voiced a shared viewpoint with which you can engage. 'It's interesting that most people thought that...' And the act of just raising an arm is ever so slightly energising. People have to listen, think, decide and then act. Better than nothing.

In making people think about a question enough to answer it, and then indicate their answer, the humble show of hands creates a dialogue between the presenter and the audience.

You can go further with the show-of-hands idea. You can turn the question into the lever for your next point. I saw a really good example of this during a series of pitch presentations at a conference on 'Smart Cities' in Paris. I had conducted a workshop with the presenters a day earlier and the subject of interaction came up. 'Important, yes,' the general sentiment seemed to be, 'but hardly practical in such a short talk.' 'But what if you were to ask a question at the start,' I suggested, 'that seeded the logic for the rest of your talk? What if you could somehow get the audience to make your point for you with their answer?' This would also have the benefit of surprising the audience who would be bracing themselves for a hurried, five-minute rant only to have things turned back on them. One guy implemented the idea brilliantly.

His business was the smart metering of electricity. He opened with the question, 'Who knows, roughly, how much their utility bill was last year?' Most hands went up. 'OK,' he continued, 'who knows what that that bill would have been for just last week?' Practically all of the hands went down, accompanied by a few wry smiles. 'Well, if you can't link your actions in a given week to what they cost you, as you would, say, with your weekly shopping, how can you manage them?' And with that, he had platformed his entire talk. He now had slightly less time to present but he was presenting to a room of people who could see the sense of what he was saying. He had buy-in.

It can be tricky to think of a question as incisive as this. You don't want to ask something too bland ('Hands up who likes food?') or something too broad ('What do people think about technology?') but asking the audience anything at all is better than not doing so. It shows that you are open to suggestions and you want to engage. It also puts a little pause into the presentation which is never a bad thing.

Level 6 – Very Mild Interaction, a Hint of Interaction

It is important to note, again, that forced interaction doesn't work. I've seen presenters ask clunky questions to liven up a poor presentation and the audience has only answered out of politeness. That's no use.

The real essence of interaction is that people are keen to interact, even if they don't speak. At its core, it is a feeling not an activity, and you can engender this feeling in many subtle ways. For example, you can ask rhetorical questions – 'So how do we do this in practice?' – which show that you are thinking the issue through with the audience and asking the same questions they will be thinking. Another thing you can do is choose examples that are relevant to the people in the room. The more the presentation is tailored to the audience, the more they will feel the presenter is talking to them and them alone, and this will inspire them to talk back. Even just good eye contact, as we saw in chapter 2, will give the presentation a conversational feel and prompt people to reply.

Presenter-Free Presentations

Sometimes, when I meet people and tell them what I do, they look at me, and I know what they're thinking. 'Presentations? You don't look the type.' And in the obvious sense I'm not. The word 'presentation' conjures up notions of showmanship and extroversion that are not my natural style. However, it suits my communication style always to try and bring the audience in, and the most coveted scenario for me is a kind of 'presenter-free-presentation' where participants are not just discussing issues with me but with each other. Not everyone is comfortable with this level of anarchy, but I know that if people are active, they are learning, which is a good thing.

So, as with everything in this book, implement the techniques that align with your own natural communication style. I love open-ended discussions, myself, but you might prefer to do things differently. Which is fine. But always be mindful of what the audience is thinking and doing, and try not to muzzle them if they actually want to speak. *Let them in.*

CHAPTER 6

Being Boring – No Topic Is Boring; Boredom Is Relative

The Problem

Your presentations are boring, your subject matter is dull and you're not a good enough communicator to make it interesting.

Except that's not the problem at all. Boredom is relative and no topic is inherently boring. Or put another way, you have to figure out which bit of your material is useful and interesting to the audience, and present only that. Due to a poor understanding of how presentations work, people fail to grasp this simple and yet vital concept.

The Reason

We already touched upon this problem in chapter 4 when we looked at overlong presentations where the speaker focuses on what he or she knows, rather than on what the audience wants to hear. And we saw another version of the same problem in chapter 5, on Interaction, where I said that presenters worry more about how well they are speaking than about how well the audience is listening. Boring presentations arise from the same misdirected focus.

People look at great speakers and try to emulate their qualities of interesting-ness. They try to speak in a way that will turn their dull mumblings into '*I have a dream*'. This completely misses the point. What makes a presentation interesting is content, not delivery. Yes delivery is important, but as we said in the last chapter, you know how to deliver. Speaking is something you have already mastered. The trick is to create content that will allow you to use this natural speaking style in all its glory.

The Solution

To figure out how to make your presentation interesting, let's look at some examples of communications that work. Some of these are one-to-one scenarios and some are one-to-many but all share a common relationship between the speaker and listeners. This can be summarised in a single phrase: *they are given by an 'expert' to an 'interested group'.* And all presentations should have the same profile.

When I say that a presentation is given by an expert to an interested group, people often raise their eyebrows. The two things presenters worry most about are:

1. Getting asked a difficult question – *not* being 'expert' enough
2. The audience dozing off – not being 'interested'.

Your first task is to figure out in what respect you are the expert relative to the audience, and what that audience is interested in. If you do this, the battle is as good as won. Fail to do so, and you may as well not present at all.

To show you what I mean, let's look at some examples. The first one we have already seen: a doctor-patient consultation. The doctor knows lots of stuff – expert – and the patient has a need – interested – and the doctor only tells the patient the things he or she needs to know to get well. The doctor will give a small amount of background theory, because an instruction alone – 'Take these pills' 'Don't eat dairy' 'Stop working' – would not be convincing without some explanation to back it up. This is true of all presentations. You won't convince someone to invest in your product if they have no clue how it works. People have to 'get it' to buy it, so there is always a transfer of at least some knowledge. Mind you, a doctor won't subject you to a PowerPoint presentation or make you read a text book, he or she will just tell you enough to achieve a tangible outcome: make you well.

Another example of this expert/interested-group profile, very much in the presentation format, is the weather forecast. The weather forecast looks simple – two minutes, friendly presenter, nice pictures – but is anything but. It is created by specialist meteorologists who gather huge quantities of data from disparate sources, process it through complex mathematical equations and computer algorithms, and present it on animated infographics and charts. The final communication is simple but that's only because of the compression, simplification and customisation that has taken place. It is a classic example of a presentation: an expert presenting just the insights the audience needs to hear.

The weather forecast encapsulates the phrase, 'boredom is relative'. It is interesting only if the weather affects you. The same is true of a presentation; you have to figure out what part of your knowledge will be interesting to the audience and present only that.

Boredom is Relative

The weather forecast also encapsulates the phrase I used earlier: boredom is relative. Is the weather forecast interesting? Well it depends on the audience. My brother-in-law always knows the weather for the coming days. Always. He lives on the Isle of Man and when he comes to visit us in Dublin, he changes the setting on his phone to get weather updates for his new location. Why? Because he is from a farming background and although he now runs his own IT company, he still maintains a smallholding and helps his father with his. To a farmer, weather sets the pattern of the day; to a farmer, weather is yield and livelihood; to a farmer, weather is everything. So it's no wonder he takes a keener interest in the weather forecast than anyone I know.

The weather, like any topic, is interesting if it affects you. If you are going sailing or having a bbq or painting the outside of your house, it's spellbinding. If you live in the city, drive to work and have to stay late tomorrow, it's not so vital. And the other interesting thing about the weather forecast is that it is tuned to its audience. It may seem simple with its cloud and sun symbols, and its wind arrows and numbers, but that is only because it has evolved this way to meet the needs of the audience. Imagine if there had never been a weather forecast and you approached a group of meteorologists and asked them to take all of their data and analytical models, and produce a two-minute presentation that a child could understand. They'd laugh at your innocence and optimism. 'Two minutes? Have you any idea how complicated this stuff is?'

The other thing to note, when you next watch the TV weather bulletin, is that there is almost no text on the screen. There are numbers, symbols and single-word captions like 'Tuesday morning', but no bullet points. The presenters don't write the weather down, they say it and they show it.

Another example of this expert/interested-group communication profile occurs in a shop. The shop assistant knows a lot about the shop's goods – wine, second-hand records, shoes, video cameras – but they will only tell you the stuff you need to know. The communication will have a tangible outcome – choose something to buy – and will (like the doctor-patient consultation) be quite short. Also, like the doctor-patient consultation, it will be interactive and personal and, given that you go into a shop of *your* own volition, not boring.

The conversation you have with a trustworthy shop assistant is
another example of a presentation.

One of my own shopping experiences brought this home to me and I have used the example many times since. I was looking for an iPod docking station which is basically a speaker for an iPod. I didn't want to spend too much money and I wasn't hugely fussy on quality, but I wanted it to be loud enough for a party we were throwing that evening. I could tell that the shop assistant was both knowledgeable and honest – he recommended the cheaper option – so I was confident I would get what I came for. And I did. Ten minutes after entering the shop I left with a bagged purchase and one less job on my to-do list.

Everything in the conversation with that shop assistant mirrored what a good presentation should be. There was an expert and an interested audience, and the conversation had a tangible goal: choose a product. The expert knew lots about music, electronics, acoustics, and Apple products but he only gave me – the audience – a small parcel of this knowledge, relevant to my goals. All of the communication tools that will be discussed later in this book were employed, namely: demonstrations, stories (from the shop assistant's own experience with the same device at home), analogies (with other similar products) and examples (prices, powers, weights). There was interaction, of course, as well as all of the obvious stuff: hand gestures, eye contact, vocal inflection and enthusiasm. And there was one more crucial element that reflects the expert/interested-group relationship: the shop assistant didn't just present information, he presented *insight*. A presentation is not just facts, it's an interpretation of facts. Your own presentation should be the same.

I remember a short presentation I saw once on films. The guy who gave the talk was a huge film buff and he told the audience, almost breathlessly, about the different movie genres, how the film industry works, his own efforts at movie-making and even his weekend movie-watching ritual. He also cited examples and played a few short clips. For 10 passionate minutes it was movies, movies, movies, before he finished and opened the floor to questions. Can you think what the first question might have been? 'What is your favourite movie?' And I'm guessing you thought of the same question yourself, because when I tell this story to other people they almost always say the same.

An audience see a good presenter and say: 'You seem to know what you're talking about and you seem interested, so what do you think? What advice would you give me?' If a friend of yours had a house in France and spent every summer in France, and you were thinking of going on holidays to France, yourself, who would you ask for advice? Even if you wanted to research the topic yourself, you would still probably ask your friend which book or website he'd recommend. Why scurry around lost at the wrong end of the communication chain when a quick steer from an expert can get you where you need to go?

Your job as a presenter is to advise and guide your audience. Time might be short but the quality of the content is high. You are taking the audience somewhere they couldn't easily get to themselves and this is extremely powerful.

One more example illustrates this idea beautifully. Consider a conversation with a solicitor. Let's say you are wondering about the legality of moving the fence between your garden and a neighbour's to facilitate an extension to your house, and you need some advice. The point is, you could access the relevant laws yourself – they are all in public records – but you wouldn't know what to do with them. Even the half-page of legalese that came with my iPod docking station was too much for me. So you need an expert to consider all of this information and pull out the key insights. Your lawyer does this and communicates it to you as succinctly as possible: 'You need to move your fence two feet to the left or you neighbour will sue you.' And you say, 'Thanks very much. What do I owe you?'

A lawyer doesn't just tell you what the laws are, he tells you what they mean.

This communication relationship – expert to interested group – occurs in all functional communications. Imagine you are out with friends having a heated discussion about, let's say, an upcoming football match. Let's imagine you all support the same team but disagree on player selection or the way the team is set out to play. And let's say you have been quiet in the conversation for some minutes, listening to other people's points or simply daydreaming. Then you hear something you disagree with so you speak up. 'No, he plays better in a 4-4-2 than he does as a lone striker… He used to play that way when he played for… As a defender, I used to find it much easier to mark someone if… I remember a game when he scored against… ' and so on. You talk for 30 or 40 seconds before concluding: 'So, I really think you have to play him in a front two,' and then you stop and someone else comes in.

For that 30 or 40 seconds you are making a presentation. You are the only one talking as several people listen. No one thinks about conversations in this way but effectively you are saying to the rest of the group: 'Everyone stop and listen to me; you need to hear this!' There's an urgency about the communication and the same urgency can, and should, fuel your presentations. Like a lawyer, you are 'advising' your clients, or better still 'strongly advising' them.

When you speak in a conversation, you are effectively saying: 'Everyone stop talking and listen to me. You need to hear this.'

Audience Focus

Lip service is paid, in presentation books, to 'knowing your audience' but this phrase is never really teased out. People plan presentations around flaccid motivations: *This topic is important; I know a lot about it; I'll talk for an hour and the audience will learn stuff.* But communication in the real-world doesn't work like that. You are not tossing information at the audience like breadcrumbs to ducks. You are taking them on a journey which leads them from a problem to a solution. I'll state again something I said earlier: it's not *information* you are giving the audience but *insight.*

I came across an interesting counter-example to this when on holiday a few years ago; an example which explains where a lot of presentations go wrong. I was staying in a hotel that had an elegant library room in which the high walls were lined with hard-back books, many very old. One was the 1959 edition of the *Encyclopaedia Britannica* and browsing this absently, I came across the following passage on Dublin, the county in Ireland where I live. I have reproduced a portion of the entry below.

Dublin, a county of Ireland in the province of Leinster, bounded north by county Meath, east by the Irish Sea, south by county Wicklow, and west by counties Wicklow and Meath. The area is 321 square miles and the population (1951) 170,839 apart from Dublin city [area 34 square miles, population 522,183]... The central and northern parts of the county are low-lying and composed chiefly of Carboniferous Limestone, with some millstone grit to the north and northwest, and some Silurian and Ordovician rocks behind Balbriggan. The peninsula of Howth, connected by a raised beach with the mainland, is formed of old quartzite and shale, crushed and folded, and probably of Cambrian age. The rocks of the county show many signs of ice action.

Does this description of Dublin strike you as odd? Have you been to Dublin? Did you know about the 'Silurian rocks' around the town of Balbriggan? Had you spotted evidence of 'ice action'? Did you know that the area of the county was 321 square miles? Is that big or small as counties go? Do you care? Have you visited Howth? I have. It's just three miles from where I live and I played football for Howth Celtic for seven years. I know many people in Howth and I've been to the harbour and the town many times, cycled Howth hill, played golf in Deer Park and walked the breath-taking cliff walk that takes you around the headland. But I confess that I didn't know anything about 'old quartzite and shale'. It's a strange account of Dublin, is it not? I wondered who on earth the target audience is perceived to be, which got me thinking.

Many presentations are guilty of being encyclopaedic, presenting large quantities of information without any thought as to what the audience will do with that information.

Suppose, like me, you're from Dublin and you meet someone on holiday who is thinking of visiting. What would you tell them? Would you tell them about the 'carboniferous limestone' or the 'millstone grit'? I doubt it. You'd more likely tell them about tourist attractions, pubs, restaurants and weather. Now, what if, rather than taking a holiday in Dublin, this person was thinking of moving there? What might you then tell them? You'd probably talk about house prices, job opportunities, schools and – once again – weather. What if they wanted to set up a business? Then it's corporate tax rates, salaries, energy costs, and so on. Dublin is many different presentations to many different people, and the encyclopaedia faces a problem because, for a general readership, it cannot know who its audience will be.

Many presentations are guilty of being encyclopaedic in the same way. Information is dispersed neutrally without much thought about the needs of the audience. The stock company presentations I castigated in the first chapter fall squarely into this category. If a presentation is designed for everyone, it will be useful to no one. You need to give the presentation an arrow-like quality, pointing somewhere the audience needs to go.

Arguing the Point

One benefit of aligning a presentation's goals with the audience's needs is that it gives you a conviction that energises your communication. We all know, from TV chefs to great teachers we had at school, that enthusiasm is infectious. Some people find it hard, though, to pump themselves up for a presentation at work, but you don't have to. Simply having a clear aim and knowing how this aim will benefit the audience gives you that conviction.

When you argue a point, as in the photograph on the right, all your communication skills – eye contact, hand gestures, vocal inflection, vocal volume, emotion, energy – kick in spontaneously.

Think again of the conversation with friends about football. When you are arguing a point, you do all of the right things from a communication point of view. Eye contact becomes fixed and intense – see the above figure – your voice is raised and inflected, your body language becomes pronounced (wagging finger, shaking head, incredulous upturned palms) and you become totally audience-focused as reflected in the use of phrases like, 'You don't understand,' or 'You're not listening.' Obviously you don't want to be apoplectic with rage when making a presentation, but having a clear purpose will make you a much more compelling and unself-conscious communicator.

The converse is also true. Inasmuch as you should try to be enthusiastic, you should also avoid being unenthusiastic. What I am talking about, here, is the tendency of nervous presenters to apologise. They apologise for slides that aren't clear; they apologise for not explaining themselves very well; they apologise before their presentation to those who have heard this stuff before; they apologise after their presentation for going over time.

Apologies are a noble and necessary thing in life but not in a presentation. If something in your presentation necessitates an apology, it shouldn't be in your presentation. If a graph cannot be seen from the back of the room, re-draw it so that it can be seen. If the room is too big for everyone to hear you, figure that out beforehand and get a microphone. If you are worried about having too much material, rehearse the presentation and ensure that you don't have too much material. And if something does go wrong despite all of this preparation, don't dwell on it anxiously, just carry on. You might have spent ages shooting and editing a video that just won't play, and that might be really annoying to you, but the audience doesn't know what they have missed. Take the setback on the chin and get on with it.

The main reason presenters apologise, of course, is nerves. It's a way of levelling with the audience – I don't want to give this any more than you want to hear it; I'm just like you – but it's actually in the interests of the audience that you succeed, not fail, so don't undersell your content with apologies, just deliver it with conviction.

Justification of the Conclusion

In many ways, a presentation can be seen as a justification of its conclusion. Other communications like reports, websites and even this book, have different sections with different takeaways, but due to its brevity and transience, a presentation should really be built around a single, clear conclusion. Essentially this is your aim: the first thing you write down and the last thing you say. The presentation will then take the audience to this conclusion.

I always use the same example to explain this – that of a phone call. Imagine you call your wife or husband or housemate, and began a conversation as follows: 'Hi, it's me, I'm calling about the party tonight.' This sets the context for the communication, that you have a message to pass on, and that you need the other person to listen. If you opened with, 'Hi, how are things?' you would be setting a different context: that you are phoning for a chat. In a presentation, you have to set this context and it will probably take more than one sentence to do so, but the introduction does the job of telling the audience where you will be taking them and why.

A telephone call, where you have a message to impart, embodies the beginning-middle-end structure of a presentation.

Next, you explain why you phoned. 'I'm going to be working late, tonight, so I'll have very little time to go home before heading to this party. So it will be easier if I go straight to the restaurant. But there's a present and a card in the drawer beside my bed which I won't be able to pick up, so will you bring that with you and I'll sign the card when I'm there.' This is the who-what-when-where-why of the communication that you go through to make everything clear. What, then, is the last thing you say before hanging up? Apart from maybe a quick conversational exchange, the last functional statement will be something like, 'So, whatever you do, don't forget the present.' This, after all, is the reason you phoned.

However, if you had called and simply said, 'Bring the present and card in my bedside drawer to the party,' and then hung up, apart from being very rude, your message would prompt an immediate return call with a slew of questions. 'What present? What drawer? Why won't you be home to get it yourself?' In other words, you wouldn't have done enough to justify the conclusion. A presentation is structured in exactly the same way.

- Decide what the aim of the presentation is – conclusion
- Tell the audience at the start where they are going and why – introduction
- Use the presentation to get them there – body

This three-part structure – introduction, body, conclusion – is often paraphrased as, 'say what you're going to say; say it; say what you've just said,' but it is more subtle than that. You are not just repeating yourself three times, rather you are moving that audience towards a conclusion that is useful to them.

Some presentations don't have a single takeaway. You may simply be trying to provoke a discussion or see if people have questions, but this is still an *outcome*. It's still something towards which the presentation can be targeted, and thinking this way will lead you to make better decisions about what should (and shouldn't) be included. In a group conversation, you only volunteer comments that you think will be relevant and interesting to the other members of the group and the same is true of a presentation. If you approach it this way, no presentation should ever be boring.

CHAPTER 7

Talking Over Their Heads – Experts Who Lose the Room

The Problem

The problem of presenters talking over the heads of the audience is a very interesting one because it is a problem most presenters don't realise they have. Which is precisely why they have it.

If you feel your material is too complex, you'll simplify it so that it is no longer too complex. Only it may still be too complex but you won't realise it. And the audience won't tell you; they'll just stare blankly, keep quiet, and probably even give you a polite round of applause at the end. You won't think your material is too complicated but chances are… it is! In presentations, it nearly always is.

The boffin at the blackboard is a well-known stereotype but the reasons behind this communication failing are subtle and varied.

On my first day in college, the third lecture was chemistry. My sister, who had studied engineering before me, said that the chemistry course was a beast but she hadn't done it at school, as I had, so I thought I might be OK. But as we descended swiftly into the murk of Schrodinger's Equation and the Heisenberg Uncertainty Principle, I started to wonder. There were squiggles on the board that I didn't recognise, but thought might be partial derivatives – denoted '∂', or possibly 'δ', or maybe even 'ξ' – but I wasn't sure, so I asked the person next to me. He said he didn't know, either, but he was pretty certain they were all the same. In other words, we could just make a mark of some sort and figure out what it meant later. At least that way we'd have a set of notes to work off. So I ploughed on, writing these mysterious doodles into my notes and thinking: *welcome to university*. Many years later, when I started training people to make presentations, I thought again about my chemistry lecturer. He was probably in his sixties and yet, after several decades of lecturing, he had learnt nothing.

That's the thing about both presentations and lectures, you could do them for years and never improve. It's a chastening thought but if you never get feedback (and many lecturers and presenters don't) then how can you improve? And although we have all seen examples like the one described above, and laughed, what I want to stress here is not how far out of touch he was, but how little he realised it. I know from experience that most people reading this book, on some occasions if not very often, are guilty of doing much the same thing but without realising it. The reasons for this mismatch between presenter and audience are poorly understood but fascinating for this very reason.

The Reason(s)

As I see it, there are three reasons why people make their presentations too difficult to understand. Just like 'caution', as discussed in chapter 3, these three things lurk in the presenter's subconscious and affect behaviour when creating content. They are a trio of mental biases which I label:

- The curse of knowledge
- A reluctance to be inaccurate
- A loss of creativity

We'll look at each in turn.

The Curse of Knowledge

I came across 'the curse of knowledge' concept in Chip and Dan Heath's really interesting book, *Made to Stick*, and although they didn't coin the term themselves, they explained it very well with interesting examples and case studies of their own. I won't rehash the discussion or the background to the idea, but it basically says that the more expert you are on a topic, the worse you are at judging how difficult other people will find it. In other words, experts think things they know are simpler than they actually are. Of course, we have all observed this, and my chemistry lecturer is a case in point, but the idea is more nuanced and more embedded in day-to-day behaviour than we think.

I often use a different phrase to describe the same phenomenon, which is: 'forgetting what it's like not to know.' Not quite as catchy as 'the curse of knowledge' but I think it's actually a more accurate description of what's going on. Learning is a process of building mental scaffolding to understand new concepts and then discarding this scaffolding when the concept becomes solid. We go from having to think our way through a new idea slowly, and in steps, to just 'getting it'.

At school, children learn mathematical concepts using simple rules-of-thumb and practice these many times until they 'get' the new concept implicitly.

In my earlier book, *The Natural Presenter*, I discussed the example of a child learning multiplication at school. My sister, who is a primary school teacher, told me that multiplication is explained by drawing an analogy with addition, which the child has already mastered. So 5 multiplied by 6 is explained as 5's added together 6 times. And division is then taught, not as multiple subtraction, but as reverse multiplication.

Everyone reading this book, however, knows what multiplication is. You don't have to think through these steps, you just 'get it'. If I ask you how much money you have in your pocket and you pull out four twenties, you do the multiplication without thinking and get 80. However, most people, when I ask them, cannot recall how they learnt to multiply or divide because they have discarded the mental scaffolding by which they learnt it long ago. This is why explaining everyday things to young children is so challenging. Once you master something, you internalise the steps that brought about that learning and do them subconsciously, and it is very hard to remember back to that temporary learning phase.

Learning mathematics, in fact, is a long chain of these bridging analogies; each one a scaffold to bring you to the next concept. When you have mastered multiplication and division, you can handle other arithmetic concepts like factors and squares. Then you can learn about number lines and two-dimensional spaces. Then you can learn about triangles, circles and geometry. Then, if so inclined, you can learn about coordinate geometry, followed by differentiation, followed by integration (reverse differentiation), and so on.

The process doesn't just apply to conceptual knowledge, either. Procedural knowledge, like learning to drive a car, is internalised in the same way. When you start driving, you have to think of 10 things at once – mirror, clutch, hand-brake, gear-stick, mirror again, accelerator, steering wheel – but when you get used to carrying out these steps in harmony, it becomes just 'driving'. You forget about the individual actions and think on a higher level: 'Traffic's very bad'; 'I'm glad it's Friday'; 'This radio programme is rubbish'. So the difficulty for experts is to discard these high-level associations and descend to a more rugged lower-level of references that a novice will comprehend. For many presenters this can be a real challenge.

Reluctance to Be Inaccurate

This is different to the last point. The curse of knowledge is a cognitive limitation, this one is behavioural. I noticed this when my technical communication course was joined, a few years ago, by a cohort of students from a professional Masters programme. This is akin to an MBA for engineers and the people doing it have 10 or more years' industry experience. I noticed that their slides and diagrams were more detailed and complex than those of the undergraduates, and even when I peddled the merits of simpler visual aids, they seemed to be a reluctant to let go.

Now, I want to leave this example for a moment and ask you a question. What is the locus of points equidistant from a fixed point 'focus' and a straight-line 'directrix', where the focus does not lie on the directrix? Any ideas? I'm guessing not many people will know the answer to this. The answer to the question is a 'parabola' and to show you what this is, I've drawn one below.

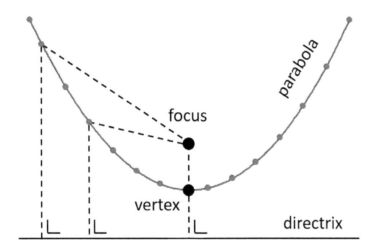

A parabola is a kind of 'U'. A 'locus' is the set of points that satisfy a particular rule and in this case the rule is that every point is the same distance from the 'focus' as the 'directrix'. Clear? Very possibly not. I know this definition because I studied the parabola in school but the definition, although correct, is not the best way to explain it to someone who doesn't know what a parabola is. What's a better way? Well, I found this out by running an exercise several times on courses where I got people in groups to explain different things, one of which was a parabola. Another shape I got them to explain was an ellipse, which is one of these: ⬭

For starters, nearly everyone draws a picture. They may sometimes draw the wrong picture but they are at least trying to visualise what's in their heads. This is yet another lesson to all the bullet point fanatics out there: visual is more direct. Then they use verbal descriptions for a parabola like, 'u-shaped', 'saucer-shaped', 'the shape of a car headlight mirror', 'half a MacDonald's M', 'the path a football takes when you kick it through the air' or 'the shape of a hanging rope held at both ends'. For an ellipse, they say, 'squashed circle', 'stretched circle', 'egg-shaped', 'rugby-ball-shaped', 'the shape of a plate when looked at from an angle' and even 'the shape of the orbit of a planet around the sun'.

No one writes equations or uses the kind of officious definition I gave of the parabola. This makes perfect sense if we remember again the idea of the communication chain. There may be a very accurate mathematical definition but you are only trying to describe it to someone at the most basic level; so a simple, direct explanation is more compelling. There is nothing wrong with equations and definitions, obviously, and when I studied engineering I had them coming out of my ears, but they are not the best way of describing a concept in the first instance. The cognitive load is too high. So show equations by all means but use familiar analogies, examples and images – rugby balls, saucers, eggs – to complement these equations.

In college, I remember opening lines from lectures like: 'Consider N arbitrary integers such that the set of all R(N) unit vectors on a Cartesian plane…' instead of, 'Imagine you hit a golf ball down a fairway and there was a cross wind…' Why don't people use these simple references in lectures and presentations, the way the same people would use them in conversations? Is it the boffin succumbing to the 'curse of knowledge' again? No, I think there is something different going on here, which I was alerted to by the engineering Masters students I mentioned earlier. It struck me that they were reluctant to simplify their material because this made it less accurate. Steeped in a profession where precise, detailed documents and protocols are essential to efficiency, reliability and even safety, it is unsettling to speak about these things in a loose and simple way. This strikes me, again, as a failure to see the difference between a short, high-level, transient presentation and a detailed follow-on document, each with its own place in the communication chain. People seem to get the difference, implicitly, in conversations, but not in presentations.

*Most of the communications people engage with at work – reports,
design drawings, 'process flow diagrams', 'standard operating procedures'
– are necessarily detailed and accurate, and against this backdrop it
can be difficult, in a presentation, to seem to speak inaccurately.*

The lecturers who taught me were succumbing to the same aversion to inaccuracy. They were teaching subjects like mechanics, materials and thermodynamics because they were specialists in these areas, so to start a course with a woolly or inaccurate statement would have felt unprofessional. It was also something they weren't used to doing in their day-to-day work.

If you think about it, all of the ellipse and parabola descriptions I got from the brainstorming exercise were, to some degree, inaccurate. A parabola is not U-shaped, it diverges continuously whereas the sides of a U rise straight up. And it's not the shape taken up by a hanging rope – although it is very close – which is actually a curve called a 'catenary'. And an ellipse is not egg-shaped because eggs are not symmetrical about both axes but pointed at one end. And it's not even, strictly speaking, like a rugby ball because rugby balls are three-dimensional whereas ellipses are two-dimensional. Rugby balls are actually 'ellipsoids'. Although this sounds picky, even facetious on my part, experts tie themselves up in knots with this kind of stuff. Really they should begin simply and add detail, but with their 'locus of points equidistant from a fixed point focus…' they are starting with the finished product and moving backwards along the communication chain.

Loss of Creativity

This is also something that worsens over time but not in the way you might think. The stereotypical view is that young people – children in particular – are creative and free-minded, middle-aged people are mature and consistent, and old people are stubborn and set in their ways. And this is true, to a certain extent, but general ageing is not the driver for the loss in creativity I am talking about. What I have noticed is that between leaving school or college, and having spent a few years in the workplace, divergent thinking diminishes and in a way that is very damaging to presentations.

Kids take an angled view on things but lose this creativity as they grow. However a similar process occurs – a loss in divergent thinking – when people go from education to the workplace and this can adversely affect their presentations.

A few years ago, I did two training courses in the same week, one in Chester in the north of England and the second in Grenoble in the south of France. The first course was with PhD students working in the area of environmental sustainability, and initially I found it hard work as the participants were reluctant to engage or ask questions. They seemed to be listening but they weren't speaking, which can be a bit of a drag. Later, though, I set them working in groups to put together short presentations and they really took to the task. The energy levels in the room shot up and the final presentations were really creative and engaging. Funny, too, in many cases.

Two days later I travelled to France where the audience was very different. These people all worked for start-up companies and, unlike the students in England, the early part of the day saw much discussion, even debate, as everyone had opinions and concerns they wished to voice. I felt things were going really well before we did a final exercise on visual aids. For this, I got groups to select and then talk around engaging images and graphics to explain what they do. The results, though, were not as captivating as the student presentations earlier in the week. There were a few fairly lame google-searched images and not much more. In one instance, a Twitter logo filled the screen and I thought it was a provocative subversion of the normally tiny icon. But when I asked the group about this, they said, no, they just didn't know how to re-scale it in PowerPoint. So there was not much creativity in the presentations despite the vibrant discussion beforehand.

This set me thinking about other instances where the presentations I'd seen in companies had been far less imaginative and diverse than presentations given by students on the courses I teach. The strange thing is that many of the people in the companies were only a few years out of college, themselves. In other words, they hadn't aged very much. And experience is supposed to make you better, not worse; it gives you confidence, knowledge, stories to tell, and practice at giving presentations. When I looked closely at the content of these presentations, though, I could see that the one thing that was lacking was creativity, and creativity is a crucial element in communication.

I spoke about this already in chapter 1. You have to think of different ways of making connections as communication is a spiky, iterative, creative process, and different audiences require different approaches. You are seeking novel ways to make complex ideas clear with pictures, videos, demonstrations, stories, examples and analogies. You are likening an ellipse to an egg or a parabola to the flight of a football. It struck me that students are still learning concepts and seem more adept at forming novel connections and thinking divergently. However, people working in a company for a few years, with stable processes and surrounded by others who understand the same things and speak the same language, have a narrower mindset in this regard. In many ways, the nature of experience and expertise is to refine your thinking – 'cut to the chase', 'get to the point', 'see the wood for the trees' – but an increased precision and efficiency in thinking can lead to a stifling of creativity, which can damage your communications.

The Solution

The good news is that this problem is easy to fix. And despite the different unconscious biases at play – 'the curse of knowledge', 'aversion to inaccuracy', 'loss of creativity' – the same solution applies in all three cases. To see how, let's look at another pair of complex presentation titles like those we saw in chapter 4:

'Group III Nitride Semiconductor Nanostructures for Photonic and Quantum Photonic Applications'

Obviously, this uses far too many specialist terms to be the first link in a communication chain, but now I want you to consider this title:

'Modelling a Smooth Elastic-Inelastic Transition with a Strongly Objective Numerical Integrator Needing no Iteration'

I'm guessing you won't understand this one, either, and nor did I, but if you read it again, you will see that unlike the first title, there are no specialist terms and no fancy words. Maybe the words 'integrator' and 'iteration' are bordering on highfalutin, but the other terms – 'elastic', 'transition', 'numerical', 'smooth' – are all straightforward.

Except they're not.

These words don't mean anything because they can mean so many things. A 'numerical integrator' is what? A calculator? A mathematical model? A milometer? A gas meter? Without specific, real-world examples, it is impossible to tell. There's no context, the words just float around in the abstract space of the presenter's mind and the audience cannot pin them down.

This failing can happen due to any or all of the three mental biases we discussed. 'The curse of knowledge' prevents the presenter from seeing how baffling 'strongly objective numerical integrators' might be to a non-expert. Likewise a professional with an 'aversion to inaccuracy' will be content with these kinds of phrases because they are catch-all, and not tied to a single under-representative example like a rugby ball or a saucer. And the 'lack of creativity' is in evidence as this title makes no novel links to any part of the real world that the listener can engage with. It's complacent and bland.

But although there are three possible reasons for a bad title like this, there is one simple solution: use examples, analogies, images, stories and demonstrations to link your topic to real world. Or put another way: speak in the concrete, not in the abstract.

Speaking in the Concrete

Good communicators speak in the concrete naturally. They are not afraid to boil things down to the simplest idea; in fact, *that's what they strive to do.*

For a magazine, recently, I interviewed former Irish 'Entrepreneur of the Year', Edmond Harty, whose business, *Dairymaster*, brings digital technology to farming, and he uses the simplest analogies to describe what he does. 'Innovation is like baking a cake,' he said to me, 'it's about putting different ingredients together – some from the mechanical side, some from the electronic side, some from software, some from farming – to make something nice. The mechanical side is a big element of what we do whereas the software and electronics are a bit like the icing, but that's actually what makes it attractive to your customer.' In the same interview he referred to a tank of milk as a safe and the marketplace as a game of football. Simple yet effective and very memorable.

For the same set of articles, I also interviewed Irish politician, Stephen Donnelly, who was lauded for his ability to demystify the financial jargon that abounded during the recession. 'One of the nice bits of feedback I get from people,' he told me, 'is they say, "We love the way you explain complicated stuff without patronising us. There's nothing missing from your explanation."' Stephen Donnelly exemplifies the idea of speaking in the concrete more than most politicians and acknowledges that it has contributed greatly to his success. Having studied engineering in college he did an economics Masters and applied the same practical thinking to this. 'I was working with really smart economics graduates and they'd say things like, "You can increase the money supply." And I'd say, "That doesn't mean anything to me. What do you mean *increase the money supply?*" And they'd say, "Well, the Fed would do this…" and I'd say: "No, that doesn't mean anything, either. Take me through what that means. Literally. Does someone go to a computer? Do they print out money? Is it physical cash that goes to the banks?" I suppose it comes from my background because engineers understand stuff in a very visceral way.'

Irish politician Stephen Donnelly ascribes much of his success to his ability to explain complex economic concepts to ordinary people in concrete language they can understand.

Great communicators always break things into pieces, simplify them, and explain them back to you in the most concrete and concise way possible. But the important point I want to make here is that we all do this in conversations, all the time. Speaking in the concrete, with examples, analogies, demonstrations, images and stories is the default in conversations. For example, you would never say to a friend something like, 'I was very ill; it interrupted my life severely; it was unprecedented by my normal standards,' but rather, 'I was white as a ghost, green at one point. I lost eight pounds, I didn't eat for four days and didn't work for a fortnight. One morning I didn't even have the strength to reach for my glass of water, which was about [points] that far away.'

Likewise, you wouldn't say of a holiday: 'The weather was clement, the local culture and cuisine were exotic and appealing, and it was agreeable economically,' but instead you would take out your phone and show photographs of the hotel, or pull up your sleeve to reveal a tan, or demonstrate with your fingers the size of the cockroach you saw by the pool. You'd give examples (prices of beer, sizes of steaks, afternoon temperatures) and analogies (comparison with hotels, beaches and golf courses in other countries you'd been to) and more than any of these, you'd tell stories. In conversations, people always communicate with crunchy concrete language and you just need to remind yourself to do the same thing in a presentation. For every point you wish to make, ask yourself: can I explain this better with a picture, video, demo, example or analogy? Can I relate it to something people know?

You'll notice that good communication in all forms, not just presentations, adheres to this principle. I'm reminded of an example, a few years back, when, in a physiotherapist's waiting room, I was flicking through a copy of *National Geographic* and came across an article on ways to slow down the human metabolism. In the future this may allow people to be put into suspended animation for space flight, or keep accident victims alive longer while awaiting transport to hospital. Analogies were drawn between the human body and an engine, and between oxygen and rocket fuel. Examples of squirrels hibernating and sharks surviving out of water were cited, and one piece of research was embellished with anecdotal detail – person, place, time – of the people who conducted it. In all, I counted ten examples, two anecdotes, and six analogies in a piece that was only 430 words long, which – to draw an analogy – is equivalent to around one page of this book.

Then I went in to see the physiotherapist and she compared the tendon in my upper thigh to a piece of rope and the muscle to a spring. She also mentioned skiers and swimmers, in comparison to the footballer that I was, and told me a story about another of her patients who had a similar injury. It was the same concrete language – stories, analogies, examples – as the *National Geographic* article and you find this in all conversations. It's only in presentations that people talk gobbledegook but the fix is very simple: speak in the concrete, not in the abstract. Always.

CHAPTER 8

Telling no stories

The Problem

Just as there are many bad presentations, there are many bad presentation books and a lot of bad presentation advice. But I have never read a book or been on a course that did not promote, in the strongest possible terms, the power of stories. 'Engage your audience with a story.' 'Tell your story.' 'Make the presentation into a story.' They all stress this point, again and again, and they're exactly right to do so. And yet presenters – without realising it – invariably decline the advice. Why?

This book is not so much about what people do wrong as why? Without understanding the often unconscious biases that affect behaviour when preparing a presentation – such as caution, bullet point obsession, a poor understanding of the communication chain, or the curse of knowledge – people put together material that is essentially unpresentable. For me, top of the list of damaging things that people do differently in presentations (compared to conversations) is that they don't tell stories. Stories are the oldest communication tool known to man and still the best.

The Reason

I have observed story-phobia in hundreds of presentations over the years but I never came across any books or papers that explained it, or even seemed to notice that it existed. So, at UCD, we did some research of our own to look into the issue.

I invited people to a free half-day presentation skills workshop, divided them into small groups and set them the task of preparing and then giving a short presentation on a topic of their choice. I videotaped each of the group discussions as well as the subsequent presentations. I said that I was interested in looking at the difference in style between conversations and presentations but I did not tell them that the real goal of the study was to look at storytelling. You may think that being videotaped would affect people's behaviour but it didn't seem to; they quickly forgot about the cameras and got on with the task.

Images from a workshop that compared how often stories were told in conversations, left, and presentations, right.

The aim of the study was to see if people told more stories in conversations than they would in presentations. So, afterwards, I went through the videos and counted the number of stories recounted. I defined a story as any instance where someone drew from their personal experience, or the experience of someone they knew, to make a contribution to the conversation. The stories varied in length. Some were as long as half-a-minute:

A friend of mine... she's living in Greece... and she married a Greek man so they had the wedding there. So beautiful. And the food – we just spent the whole five days eating and eating. I came home half a stone heavier. Everything had garlic in it or fish or tzatziki... so I could talk about food for five minutes.

Others were just a sentence or two:

I went to Cyprus once... and Turkey. That's not the same, though.

I drew timelines of the conversations (around half-an-hour in length) and the presentations (around five minutes long) and marked the incidence of each story with a black line. A comparison of the two is shown in the graph below.

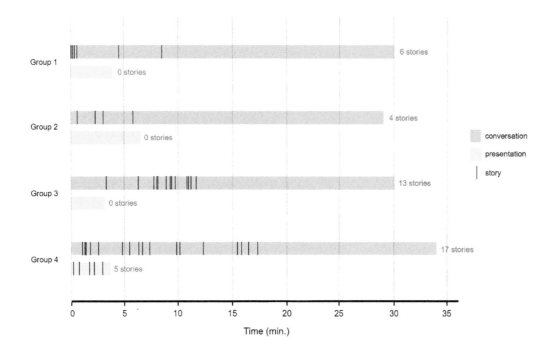

The graph shows the use of stories – each story represented by a black line –
in conversations as compared with presentations.

It can be seen that there are many stories in the small-group discussions but none in all but one of the presentations. And the presentation that did contain stories was about the different group members' experiences of coming to Ireland – they all came here to study from abroad – so that topic was personal by default and the use of stories unavoidable. But in the three presentations on abstract topics – 'potatoes', 'coffee' and 'how to make a presentation' – there were no stories at all!

This did not surprise me but I wanted to get a better handle on why it was. So I looked at the literature – educational, psychological, communications – on storytelling and what I found, to cut a long story short (pardon the pun) is that stories serve two main functions: a 'meaning-making' function and a 'social interaction' one. Or put another way, they help us to understand stuff and they help us to understand, or know, the person who is telling us that stuff. The absurd thing, though, is that people were telling stories in the small groups to help each other understand things but then not using the same stories to help the wider audience understand the same ideas in the presentations. Which makes no sense, when you think about it. Understanding the purpose of stories still doesn't explain why they should be used in one form of communication, conversations, and not in another, presentations.

A clue to what's happening here comes from the position of the stories on the timelines. First you'll notice the stories occur at the start of the conversations and then die out. This is because the latter half of these sessions are largely taken up with preparing slides and practicing delivery, so the conversations have moved on from their initial exploratory phase and the stories are no longer as necessary. The second thing to notice, though, is that the stories come in clusters, with three or four in quick succession. You should be familiar with this phenomenon in conversations where one person tells a story and this immediately prompts someone else to share one of their own. 'My brother-in-law was telling me…' 'Oh, yeah, the same thing happened to a friend of mine…' 'Well, I remember once…' and so on.

'Really? That happened to me.' In conversations, one story prompts another
but this story-chaining is missing in a one-sided presentation.

This story-chaining in conversations is so natural we take it for granted. In a presentation – which is effectively a planned conversation – it gets lost. I see this when I urge presenters to use stories in their presentations and they say things like, 'Oh, I'm not a good storyteller.' The point is, we are all good storytellers, we just don't notice it. We tell stories so often and so effortlessly, prompted by the stories of others, that we don't see a story as a valuable device that needs to be deliberately scheduled into our presentations. In fact, people are more likely to see stories – when we think about them at all – as irrelevant digressions, something personal and trite. The truth is, though, that stories are the best communication tool of all. They are better than the slideshow it took you ages to piece together, better than the video you had to ask a friend to edit, better than the research you carried out and the graphs you drew, better than the handouts you prepared and printed and copied. And the great thing is, unlike all of those other pieces of content, the preparation time for a story is practically zero. And delivery is easy.

There is, though, undoubtedly another reason for the absence of stories in presentations. Rearing its ugly head once more is the spectre of 'caution'. Of all the communication tools I urge people to use – examples, analogies, stories, demonstrations, images, videos – stories are the most susceptible to caution's scythe. And it's easy to see why. It's bad enough having to get up in front of a group of strangers, but to then have to tell them personal things about yourself and share your opinions, well that just seems like a step too far. Group conversations are far less daunting than presentations and, as we discussed in chapter 2 on eye contact, you get all of the enthusiastic nods and 'yes I see's that entice you to share your stories. But the need for stories – helping the audience understand both your topic *and you* – is just as great in a presentation as it is in a conversation. Now, let's look at different types of stories you can easily tell without feeling you are bearing all in a courtroom or on a TV chat show.

The Solution

In a lecture, once, I held up a clear, re-sealable, plastic bag containing four small pink pills and asked if anyone wanted one. There were a few frowns and a few smiles and some subdued laughter, then a longish silence before one guy asked, 'What do they do?' 'They make you feel better,' I replied, and that drew more smiles and more frowns and some shifting in seats.

Everybody takes pills, probably as often as every month. And yet these students weren't keen on taking any from me. But when a doctor scribbles an incomprehensible script, or a pharmacist goes into the back of his or her shop to fetch tablets, you don't bat an eyelid.

The point being: the source is everything. From me, or a friend, or a stranger on the street, taking pills is one thing, but from a doctor or a pharmacist it is another thing entirely.

The pills I had, by the way, were anti-inflammatories for the football injuries I incurred when I could run fast enough to get injured. So they do, in a sense, 'make you feel better' as I said. The point I was making, though, was that taking pills from stranger is like taking ideas from a presenter; if you don't trust the source, you won't trust what they are saying. Many presenters mistakenly put the facts first and hide themselves in the background. But as we said in chapter 6, you are not selling information, you are selling insight. Information is plentiful and portable but the insight of an expert is valuable. The audience must trust that expert and they cannot do this if they don't know who you are.

The main role of stories in presentations – apart from making them enjoyable and memorable – is to bring your experience to bear on what you are saying. Think of every job advertisement that's ever been written and ask yourself what is in all of them? Experience. They all want to know about your work experience and what you have done before, and the audience at your presentation is no different.

Traditionally the words of the 'wise old man' are valued because, with more experience of the world, he has more useful stories to tell. Similarly your own experience, as reflected in your stories, is the most valuable thing you can present.

On the very first presentation skills course I gave, a woman made a short presentation on Puerto Rico. She indicated its location on a map, told us facts and figures about its population, climate and culture, and even ran through a brief history of the country. At the end, someone asked her why she chose the topic, and she replied, 'Oh, I went there on my holiday last month.' She might have mentioned that. And when she returned, relaxed and bronzed from her holiday in Puerto Rico, I'm sure the first question she was asked by a friend was something like, 'How was it?' and almost certainly not, 'What is the capital city?' I could give a presentation on Puerto Rico, anyone could, but if you have actually been there, you have something more valuable to say. You have a deeper level of knowledge. Stories from your topic-related experience are how you tap into this deeper knowledge. Here are some tips on how to do this.

Start a conversation. We talked about the power of interaction in chapter 5 and it applies here too. If your presentation is more conversation-like, you will find it easier to tell stories and so will your audience when they get involved: 'Just when you said that, it reminded me of a time…' and so on. But there's another way conversations can be used to generate stories and that's in the preparation phase. If you chat through your ideas with a colleague or a friend, in explaining it to them – just like the groups in the videotaped workshop I conducted – you will undoubtedly use stories. Then you can harvest these stories and retell them in the presentation.

Tell other people's stories. A large proportion of the stories we tell in conversations are not about us at all. 'My friend was telling me…' 'My wife's sister…' 'Did you hear that guy on the radio…' We've been learning from other people's stories for thousands of years and if they enthralled you, they will enthral your audience, as well. And the great thing about second-hand stories is that someone else can be in the limelight instead of you. They'll never know.

Make the presentation a story. Rather than the story being just an episode within a presentation, the whole presentation can be an unfolding story. This can be spellbinding. The best example I saw was a woman who was explaining her research in photonics, and one bizarre application where she had to fit special glasses to jetlagged racehorses who were competing in both hemispheres in the same season. So it was a pretty good story to start with, but she told it brilliantly. 'I got an email last spring…' (screenshot of email) '…he asked me about…' (close up of highlighted sentence) '…later I went to visit the stud farm…' (photograph of farm, photograph of owner) '…he explained the problem to me…'

(picture of racehorse), and so on. There is a magic when you tell a story that I have observed many times in lectures. Pens stop writing, eyes raise to meet yours, silence descends and every expression reads the same question: what happened? Running this suspense through your presentation by making it into a single story is a very powerful technique and not too difficult to implement.

Start with a story. People often ask me for advice on the best way to start a presentation. 'I'm fine once I get going, but at the start I feel so flustered.' The perfect solution is a story. Not only will it engage the audience right from the off, and not only are the rhythms and cadences of a story easier on the ear than facts and definitions, but the story will keep you going unaided for that first minute or so. A story may run for hundreds of words and a dozen or more sentences but it is a single 'mental chunk'; it takes up just one slot in memory. In your guide notes, there will be a simple prompt, 'story: racehorses', and the next minute is taken care of. If someone were to arrive late and ask you to tell the story again, the words and sentences would all be in a different order but it would still be the same story. There are other mental chunks, apart from stories, that you can use to begin your presentation. For example, you could put up a striking image and talk around that, or read out a quotation, or do a demonstration, or state an interesting fact, or pose a question. These are all good approaches but none are as easy to prepare, easy to remember, or interesting as a story!

Personalise. Even for points where you don't have a full story to tell, try to put 'I' into your sentences. Remember that you are there to advise and enthuse the audience, so don't be afraid to state your opinion. If you say things like 'I always found this fascinating…' or 'When I get asked about this, I often say…' it shows, without a fully-fledged anecdote, that you are immersed in the subject. It shows that you have experienced your topic directly and this is how it made you feel. It's interesting to reflect that in science education you are instructed to write reports in the third-person voice – 'The potassium phosphate *was weighed* and placed in the pipette. A flame *was applied* until a bubbling of the solution *was observed*.' – as if the experiment were carried out by robots. But in a presentation, if you hide behind your material and try to let it talk for you, no one will listen.

It can seem strange to presenters but the most interesting thing about your topic is you and your stories.

I'd like to make one last point about stories. I wouldn't normally have strict rules-of-thumb about presentations, on how long they should be or how many slides you should use or where you should stand or how you should start. Every presenter is different and so is every audience and every topic. However, I would be prescriptive enough to say this: if you go through your presentation and there isn't a single story, you're almost certainly doing something wrong.

CHAPTER 9

2-D Presentations – Overlooking the Humble Demo

The Problem

For presentations I am critiquing, I often draw up a table on which I note instances of the communication tools I have highlighted in this book – stories, analogies, demonstrations, examples, images, videos, graphs – and one column is nearly always empty: 'demonstrations'. But, like interaction, live demonstrations are one thing that distinguishes a presentation from every other mode of communication. And yet presenters are so obsessed with the screen and the screen alone, they generally overlook this valuable communication tool.

The Reason

The problem here is reflected in the language people use. They call a presentation a 'PowerPoint presentation' or sometimes just a 'PowerPoint'. We looked at the issue in chapter 1, whereby presenters use the screen as a plan before the presentation, a prompt during it, and a set of notes afterwards. The screen dominates their thinking at all stages.

I earlier mentioned a friend of mine, John, who gave the presentation on 'optical packet switching' with broken pieces of colouring pencil and a hand-drawn sketch. John told me another story about a conference he went to in California where he decided not to use a slideshow at all. Instead he planned to employ a technique he had utilised successfully before, where he would draw a diagram in slow, simple steps on a flip-chart.

The interesting part of the story, though, was when John went to register for the conference on the first day. The organiser who was taking his details and preparing his name badge asked him for a memory stick or CD with his 'PowerPoint' on it. John told her that he didn't have one and he said he'll never forget the look of utter incredulity on her face. *This idiot,* she was obviously thinking, *has come all the way from Ireland to this huge tech conference in Silicon Valley, to make a presentation… without a presentation! How stupid can a person be?* John didn't disabuse her of her scorn, but simply thanked her, took his badge, and went and gave what I imagine was an excellent presentation. Most people, however, feel very naked without a detailed set of slides.

The obsession with the screen – and therefore a reluctance for doing live demonstrations or engaging the audience – is a bad habit. Beset by caution, people end up taking a conservative tack and copying what everyone does. With *their* PowerPoints. The problem we tackle in this chapter, though, is not slideshows and PowerPoint – which can be very effective – but rather the use of visual aids when a more compelling and effective live demonstration could be employed instead.

The Solution

Have a look at the images below. What do you see? An anatomical drawing of a joint? Which one? And what do the images show: direction of movement, relationship between bones, tendons and ligaments, the relative sizes of different elements, the locations of particular elements on which you might wish to carry out surgery? To show these things, you would probably need coloured arrows or outlines or enhanced shading. At the very least you'd have to do a fair bit of pointing and explaining to lead the audience – as the expert presenter always should – to the conclusions you wished them to draw.

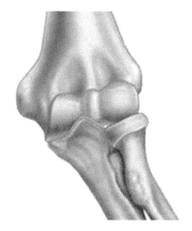

In fact, the two images are of different joints entirely: on the left a knee and on the right an elbow. I imagine that most people wouldn't have known this and the reason I showed these images is that I have seen scores of biomedical presentations over the last 15 years and I have seen many images on slides like the ones above. These are fine and necessary but there is another communication tool that nearly all the presenters ignored. It's pretty obvious, isn't it? We all have elbows and knees: three dimensional, animated, slow-motion if necessary, multi-camera angle, interactive demonstrations that blow away the kind of abstraction shown in the above diagram.

And you can take it further.

Not only does the presenter have an elbow, so does everyone in the audience. So you could ask each person to stretch out an arm, feel along the back of the bone in the wrist to find a particular joint, show motion ranges and articulations that relate to the pathology or surgery you are describing, and in doing so let the audience not just see a context for your presentation, but feel it. Like the examples and analogies we discussed in chapter 7, this doesn't negate the need for complex diagrams or mathematical equations, it *complements* them. It adds a layer or sets a context that aids the technical description enormously. And it's absurd – although I've seen this so many times – to have a picture of something when you could actually just show the real thing.

In regard to demonstrations, a recent set of talks brought home to me, very starkly, three things. Firstly, demonstrations are very effective. Secondly, demonstrations are easy to include and usually reduce your preparation workload. And thirdly, presenters miss the most blatant opportunities to include them.

It was a series of presentations given by engineering students at the end of a semester-long communications course, which was particularly rich in demonstrations. First there was the levitating ping-pong ball. You might expect, when you put a table-tennis ball in the jet stream of a hairdryer that it will fly across the room but it doesn't, it levitates magically as shown in the image below even when you tilt the hairdryer slightly. This piece of sorcery is actually called the Bernoulli Effect and is the same phenomenon that causes airplanes to lift off the ground and keeps racing cars stuck to the track.

A ping-pong ball levitating above a hairdryer: a practical
demonstration of the Bernoulli Effect.

And if you don't have a hairdryer handy, there's an even simpler demonstration you can do of the same effect by blowing across the top of a strip of paper which, surprisingly, forces the paper to lift upwards (instead of pushing it away). It's hard to explain this in words; I'd really have to show you. Which is kind of my whole point. And to back these demonstrations up, the presenters cited some real-world examples of the Bernoulli Effect like those shown in the figure below.

Further examples of the Bernoulli Effect to go with the hairdryer demo: an airplane wing and the spoiler on a race car, each producing forces but in opposite directions.

The next group gave a short talk on the gyroscopic effect and did a demonstration where the presenter, seated in a rotating office chair, tilted a spinning bicycle wheel thus causing the chair to turn. Then he demonstrated some modern applications of gyroscopes such as the tilt-sensing devices in tablets and phones. And just like the honey demonstration I mentioned in chapter 1, even though this was something people in the audience had all seen before, it took on fresh intrigue when presented in the light of these new insights. And there were further examples, such as how the gyroscopic effect can be used to tilt airborne motorcycles and even steer space stations. Obviously we didn't have a live demonstration of these but there were video clips which are the next best thing.

The last in this set of presentations was on the Coriolis Effect, a concept relating to the unusual forces experienced by objects moving on other objects which are themselves rotating. For this presentation the audience was treated to weather maps, spinning tops, and a very novel demonstration whereby the three speakers walked to different locations in the room at different speeds. Then they finished with a famous clip from the TV show, *The Simpsons,* where Bart wants to find out if water flushes down the toilet the same way in Australia as America.

These demonstrations were extremely effective and memorable. They were also, by and large, very easy to carry out and generally reduced preparation time. Think of all the complicated diagrams, images and PowerPoint animations that would have to be pieced together to explain the same concepts, and not do so as effectively.

But what struck me most about the demonstrations was their absence in other presentations I had seen in the very same room. We were in a lecture theatre where I had attended, as an undergraduate student, a great many lectures on the same topics. But in four years of detailed, complex, theory-filled classes, I had seen no demonstrations like these. Not one. No spinning tops, no bicycle wheels, no office chairs, no hairdryers. These were 36-hour lecture-courses which were totally abstract and featured no demonstrations and very few of the other communication tools we have discussed, such as stories, examples, analogies, images and videos. Somehow, it just never occurred to the lecturers.

Lectures and Presentations

The above actually made me think about the whole concept of a lecture. It's a word with a negative connotation when you think about it. 'Don't lecture me!'

And the term 'lecturer' is equally odd.

Universities want to educate students but the assumption seems to be that you do this by means of lectures. Often lecturers don't think they are doing their job if they're not talking for the whole class. Time isn't given over to demonstrations or group-discussions or in-class exercises for fear that the material won't be fully covered. But what on earth does the term 'cover' mean? When a lecturer says that he or she has 'covered' something, all they are really saying is that they have said something out loud in a room full of people. Whether the students have learnt anything is incidental. It reminds me of the riddle: 'If a tree falls in the woods, does it make a sound?' Similarly, 'If a topic is 'covered' in a room of indifferent students, is it actually covered?'

In fairness, third level education is changing. Lecturers are required to write down 'learning outcomes' for courses, and these learning outcomes have to be student-centred not topic-centred. This shifts the emphasis from what the lecturer does to what the students do. But the format of lectures hasn't changed very much and most academics are still 'lecturing' their way towards these learning outcomes.

The same is true of most presentations, possibly because of the example set in universities. Presenters tend not to think outside of the two dimensions of the screen and demonstrations are invariably overlooked. This is a missed opportunity, added to which demonstrations take less preparation time than slides and are easier to talk around.

Abstract Demonstrations

There is one more very important point to make about practical demonstrations: you don't have to demonstrate the specific physical thing you are talking about, you can demonstrate a concept or an idea just as easily. It's simply about having a three-dimensional object that you can point at, pick up, and pass around; to engage the audience on more sensory levels than just an image on a screen, or worse, text on a screen.

Most of the demonstrations I have mentioned so far – bicycle wheels and hairdryers – were used to explain physical processes, but I have seen many more that have been used to explain abstract concepts. For example, I saw a presentation on how Google search engines work, where the group members used the rows of benches in the room, and the seat numbers along these benches, to represent memory locations. Then they handed out different coloured pieces of paper with numbers and letters written on them to demonstrate how information is stored, ranked and retrieved. They also did live searches based on suggestions from the audience and showed other searches they had recorded with screen-captures. It was extremely enlightening – I'd always wondered how Google works; now I know – with the added benefit of involving the audience which always makes a presentation more memorable.

In another presentation on the depletion of the ozone layer, the presenters tied coloured balloons together to represent the chloroflourocarbon (CFC) molecules you find in aerosols. They chose appropriate colours for the atoms – green for chlorine, brown for carbon, black for fluorine – and filled the balloons with helium so that when the time came to 'release' the demo, the molecule magically rose to the ceiling as if through the atmosphere. It sounds simple – it was simple – but it was incredibly potent and memorable. And in all the years I'd studied chemistry, no one ever thought of using balloons as atoms. The group also used cardboard discs with grooves cut in them, which fit together jigsaw-like with other discs, to represent chemical reactions. The presentation was about things you cannot see – molecules – and concepts that are abstract – chemical reactions – and yet it was rich in practical demonstrations.

In a similar vein, I have seen plastic bags filled with crumpled pages to show how tummy-tuck operations work, I've seen Jenga blocks used to explain why the banks collapsed, I've seen locked lunchboxes within larger locked lunchboxes to demystify the concept of encryption, I was wowed by an agile tennis-ball-caught-on-moving-skateboard demo of

Einstein's theory of special relativity and I've had the psychological concept of 'participatory enhabituation' – no less – explained to me by means of two people balancing on a see-saw. And going back to the biomedical presentations I mentioned at the start, there is one more demonstration tool you can use: yourself.

Sometimes you can use yourself as a demonstration.

The above figure shows a woman giving a presentation on aircraft stability where she uses her outstretched arms as banking, turning, vibrating wings to fly the audience through a demonstration that a thousand diagrams could never match.

In fact, you can physically represent any concept in all sorts of ways if you put your mind to it. It may not always be necessary or easy to do, but you should really entertain the idea for a few minutes in case it is. In the long run, it will save you a lot of effort in preparation and your audience a lot of effort in comprehension.

CHAPTER 10

Graph Death – Pain but also Power

The Problem

Graphs that no one understands. Which is most graphs. You'll notice in the Q&A after a presentation that questions frequently hark back to the graphs. 'On the plot you showed… what was on the y-axis again?' I have done counts, myself, in technical presentations of how many of the graphs I fully understood in the time they were displayed, and I would estimate the success rate, conservatively, to be around 10-15%. They nearly always produce uncertainty if not outright mystification.

So don't use them? Of course not. Graphs and infographics are extremely powerful as they take numbers and turn them into shapes. This produces a form that our extremely sophisticated visual system can feast on. A table of numbers is patternless because the only way to spot a trend is to memorise numbers, and differences between numbers, for comparison purposes as you read down columns and across rows – which takes overwhelming cognitive effort.

Plot these numbers on a graph, however, and you can see correlations, kinks, upturns, downturns, intersections and slopes immediately, and to a very fine degree. The problem, though, is that the audience needs to know what they are looking at and (again) this is where there seems to be a perceptual gap between the speaker and listeners.

The Reason

The problem is not graphs, per se, but poorly explained graphs or poorly drawn ones. The expression 'as the graph clearly shows' is rarely true but in it lies the clue to what is going wrong. The speaker thinks the graph 'clearly shows' things because he or she sees the graph as they would an image. Images and graphs are both visual forms but an image is a direct copy of the physical world, an imprint of light on film, whereas the appearance of a graph depends on many factors that can drastically change what the audience sees.

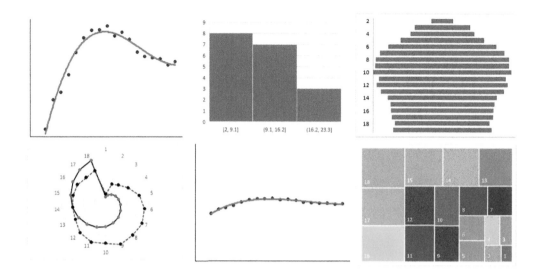

Six very different graphs plotted from the same set data set.

In the above figure, all six graphs are plotted from the same set of data and yet they present totally different appearances to the viewer. However, presenters work from the inside out. They know the point they are trying to make and select and format a graph to make this point. The audience, though, is working from the outside in, from the visual they see to the insight they are supposed to conclude. So if the visuals vary wildly, so can the conclusions drawn about them. Presenters think that everyone is seeing the same thing that the presenter is seeing, as if they are viewing a photograph, but with a graph it's never that obvious.

I'd like to take this point a step further because I know many people just don't get it. Even when I warn presenters about the confusion even simple graphs can cause, they are prone to complacency. So you might think that the point I made with the above figure is a little crude and assume that you are more controlled and clear. But even when you have a well-established template – same graph type, same scales, same interpolation of data points, same data – what you want the audience to take from the graph *and what the audience actually takes from it* may not be the same.

For example, the data set from the earlier figure is plotted below, this time identically in each of four cases. However, the conclusion drawn is different in each case. If these graphs were of, say, monthly rainfall, and you were building a reservoir for drinking water, you would be interested in the average value – top left – to work out how much water your reservoir will hold. However, if you were designing flood drains, you would be more interested in the peak rainfall – top right – to work out if they could cope with the heaviest downpour conditions. So you need to not only explain the assumptions behind how the graph works, but also what you want the audience to conclude from it. Or put another way, a picture – or a graph – is worth a thousand words, but which of those thousand words do you want the audience to hear?

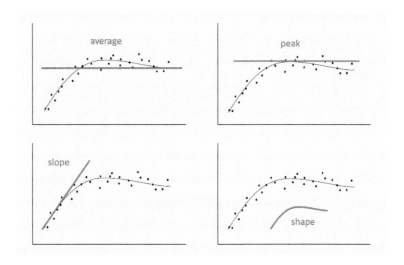

A single graph can offer many different conclusions to the viewer.
You have to spell your particular conclusion out.

So the real problem with graphs is not their use, but their *ab*-use. There is a tendency for presenters to assume that everyone sees the world the same way they do. Even if this were true – which it isn't – in the case of a graph, the audience cannot know what the shapes they are viewing tell them unless you spell things out very slowly and very clearly.

The Solution

I will not do a detailed treatment of the many different graphs you can draw, from Gantt charts to box-plots, because there are whole books devoted to the subject, many very good;

for example, those of Alberto Cairo and Edward Tufte. Here, I will just present three simple ideas to guide you in the use of graphs.

Go Slow

I heard a consultant once say: make it so simple that a child could understand it, but I don't agree with this. An audience of specialists can understand graphs that would mean nothing to non-specialists, let alone the child of a non-specialist. So simplicity is not the critical factor with graphs, slowness is. And clarity. You can build up a complex graphic but you have to introduce the rules and assumptions for doing so, one by one. In this regard, PowerPoint can really help.

Most people put up the finished graph and explain it – or don't explain it – but in so doing, you have probably already got ahead of yourself. Instead, consider the set of plots below. These could be introduced, one by one, on consecutive slides in PowerPoint, even without in-slide animations.

The first (top left) would be used to explain what the graph will aim to show. It's no harm to talk the audience through this with nothing on the screen. Then (top middle) you might explain what is on each axis, including clarifications on scale and zero offset. You could then explain what each individual point means, and show one. Following this you could show the full set of data points (top right) followed by the trendline you fitted to them (bottom left) and any assumptions you made in doing this. Then you could add in visual highlighters (bottom middle) to draw attention to particular features of the graph. Finally, (bottom right) you might overlay the graph with other comparison plots to put the results in context.

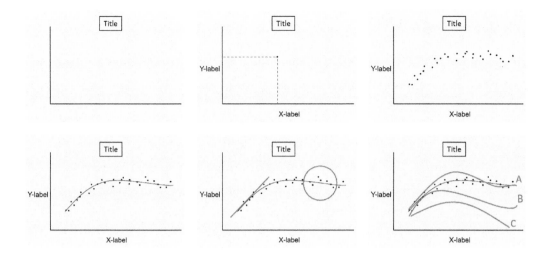

Build up the rules of your graph in slow, simple steps, explaining each step clearly to the audience.

The last plot in the above sequence indicates one of the real strengths of a graph when used properly. Once you have set the context and explained the rules of the graph clearly, you can then view many plots together or in sequence, to show trends or differences. It is easy to see even small differences between plots – in value, shape, slope – because you are using your powerful visual system. This is a neat cognitive trick, because instead of jumping between different indisciplined graphs – different types, unclear labels, shifting scales – which presents a conceptual challenge to the viewer, you are jumping between different shapes on a stable background which presents a visual challenge. This is a challenge the viewer finds much easier to accomplish. Think of how you might flick through a stack of photographs in just a few minutes; we're good visually.

The key, then, is not to dumb down but just go slow, ponderously even. Or at least that's how it will feel to you, but for the audience it takes time to understand what needs to be understood to make sense of even the simplest graph.

So once again, go slow. In case I didn't mention that.

Use Gestalt Associations

This sounds more complicated than it is and can probably be paraphrased as: 'try to keep your visual associations as intuitive as possible', or more simply, 'make things look like what they are'.

As I said earlier, I don't want to get swamped in the theory of graphic design and how the visual system works, but it would be remiss of me not to mention these concepts in passing. Gestalt psychology explains how the mind makes sense of the fragments of visual information that are thrown at it. There are principles such as:

- Closure – if the mind can form a coherent shape, it will
- Proximity – the mind will consider things that are close together to be grouped
- Similarity – the mind will consider things that are similar, in shape or colour for example, to be grouped. There are examples of each of these in the figure below.

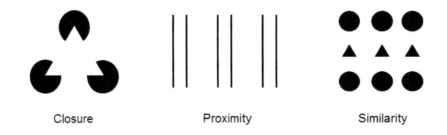

| Closure | Proximity | Similarity |

Gestalt principles of visual association. Left, you close the space between disparate objects to see a coherent shape. Centre, you see 'three pairs of parallel lines' rather than 'six lines' because of their proximity. Right, you see three rows of similar objects rather than three columns of dissimilar ones.

Putting this into practice couldn't be simpler. In fact, I have used the principles in the figure above. For instance, I put a larger distance between the three examples than I did between the features within each example so you would see them as three distinct cases. Also, I put the labels – 'Closure', 'Proximity', 'Similarity' – close to each sample so they would be associated with that sample. It's a very simple concept but often people are careless. For example, they use legends when they could make things clearer by labelling plot lines directly – proximity – and in the same colour as the plot line – similarity – as shown in the figure below.

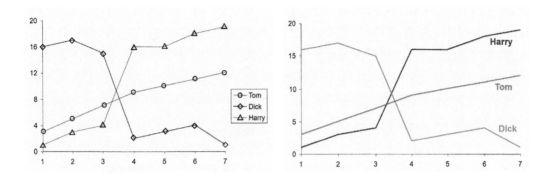

A graph with a legend on the left, and with more direct, intuitive labelling of plot lines on the right.

Besides not using these visual associations positively, often presenters use them negatively without realising it. I saw a presentation where the speaker showed a graph with three colours – red, blue, green – representing, 'sales', 'gross profit', 'net profit' and in the very next graph there were three more plot lines – red, blue, green (once more) – showing sales in 'Europe', 'America' and the 'UK'. For the speaker this was a seamless leap but for the audience it was completely jarring. The two graphs, from the back of the room, looked visually twinned but they referred to two entirely different concepts.

This often happens because people draw the graphs in Excel and the plot-lines take the first three colours that Excel assigns them. And Excel makes other decisions on your behalf, as well, such as auto-scaling the axes which can alter the relative appearance of consecutive plots. What you have to realise is that the presentation is a communication exercise, not a mathematical one. Your job is not to produce graphs and put them on the screen, your job is to create coherent visual arguments that transmit your ideas with integrity and clarity to the audience.

Don't let Excel colour and scale and format your graphs. Do it yourself.

Which brings up a very interesting point. You may have looked at the way, in the last figure, I replaced the legend for the graph on the left with direct labelling of the plot lines on the right, and wondered how I did this in Excel? Or any other graphing package? The truth is I didn't do it in Excel, I did it in PowerPoint. I copied the original plot – having first thickened and re-coloured the lines – into PowerPoint and added text labels and changed the y-axis so that it was in steps of 5 units (instead of 4), as this is much easier to interpret. I would have found it very difficult to do these things in Excel so I brought the graph into PowerPoint where I could do them more easily. The figure below shows a more extreme example of the same process.

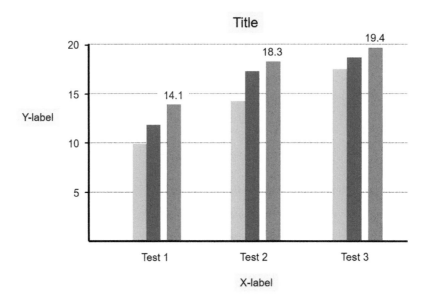

This graph uses Gestalt principles of 'similarity' and 'proximity' liberally.

The graph is from a project I worked on in the early 2000's – the title and axis-labels have been changed – where I couldn't get Excel to do the things I wanted graphically, so I constructed the graph from scratch in PowerPoint. I drew lines, text boxes and different coloured rectangles, and then used the on-screen cursors to scale the bars to the right length. You might think this lacks accuracy but you have to remember this is a *visual argument*, and if you can be as precise as people can discern from the back of a room – it's pretty easy to be – then you are being precise enough. In any case, I put the key numbers above the relevant bars to remove any uncertainty.

With complete freedom in how I format the graph, you can see that I have been able to use the Gestalt principles of association liberally. There are three tests, suitably distant from one another. Within each test, there are three values, represented by two blue lines on the left and one red line on the right. It is also obvious that the two blue lines are paired, as they are next to one another, whereas the red line is slightly removed. To further accentuate the grouping, the two shades of blue represent different versions of the same thing – in this case, for what it's worth, a refrigeration system with and without an economiser – and the red line is a totally different system.

This kind of graph can be fiddly and time consuming to produce, but once you have created the template, you can use it again and again for other sets of data. Also, I find that when you are clear about what you wish to communicate, although it may increase your workload in the time it takes to draw a particular graph, it reduces your workload insofar as you only present the important results. Bad presenters show graph after graph indiscriminately, whereas good ones figure out what the key conclusion is and present only that. In other words, you'll spend longer on each graph but present fewer of them.

Think Beyond the Obvious

I came across one study which said that 80% of all charts used by consulting firms were of just four types: bar, pie, waterfall and column. In academia I know that scatter plots and bar charts predominate. And you might argue that this makes sense as people are more likely to understand a few familiar formats. However, as I hope you appreciate from the early part of this chapter, even a simple XY graph can have many different interpretations. So resorting to a few standard forms may actually lead to complacency rather than clarity.

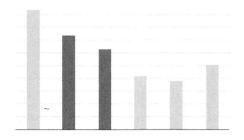 

Many standard graphic formats are used out of habit, despite their shortcomings. The bold areas of each of the above graphs show the same two numbers but the relative comparison is much easier in the bar chart than the pie-chart, demonstrating a weakness of the latter.

As an example, consider the above figure which shows the same six numbers plotted on a bar-chart (left) and pie-chart (right). As you can see, the bar chart makes it much easier to compare different quantities such as the two bars that are highlighted, which appear almost identical on the pie-chart. The point I want to make is that most people don't realise the limitations of, say, pie-charts and, as a consequence, you see them everywhere. So despite how standardised and universally understood you think a particular graph is, it may not be very effective and you should always ask yourself: is this really the best way to present my data?

Due to the brevity of a presentation, your graphics have to be quite simple but this actually frees you to do some really creative things. Remember, a graph is just a way to make numbers visual, and if you reflect on this every time you have numbers to present, it should prompt you think beyond the obvious and create clear and memorable infographics.

Consider the figure below which shows two slides from a presentation on Compressed Air Energy Storage, or CAES for short. CAES is a technology for storing excess electricity – created by renewable energy sources such as wind and solar – whereby the spare energy is used to compress air and pump it into underground salt caverns. Then, at times when the wind is not blowing or the sun shining, you extract the compressed air back through turbines and regenerate the electricity.

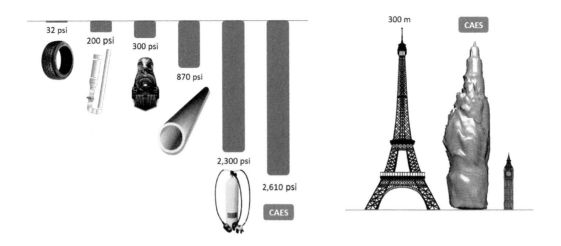

You are free to create any visual argument you wish, to show your data as clearly as possible. Above is a creative example.

The graphic on the left of the figure was used to give an idea of just how high the pressure in these salt caverns is and pretty much speaks for itself. The length of each bar is proportional to the pressure and each picture represents a real-world example of that pressure. It should also be noted also that these elements were introduced one by one. The graphic on the right gave an idea of the size of the salt caverns. The central image is a 3D geological scan of an actual cavern and it is flanked by two extremely familiar visual analogies. If the speaker were giving the presentation in America, he might use the Empire State Building or the Statue of Liberty instead. The point is, you could say these numbers, or write them down in bullet points, or put them in a table, or even plot them on a standard graph, but it's hard to imagine a clearer rendering than the one shown above. With just a little bit of thought and a few minutes of image-searching, you can produce something unique, engaging and memorable.

Below is an image from a presentation on supermarket advertising. For this, the presenters went to a local shop, took photographs, interviewed the store manager, surveyed customers and even snatched a few pricing labels like the one shown below. They analysed fonts, colours, text sizes and layouts, and one of the points they wanted to make was that the amount of money the customer saved was more prominently featured on the advertisement than the price of the item. This is obvious from looking at the ad, but as a nice extra touch, they added the two tape-measures to put an exact figure on the difference and even compared this ratio of sizes to that found in another shop. What I particularly liked was the precision and attention to detail, in that the group realised the ad would be shown on screen and therefore not to scale, so the tape measures were added to tie the numbers back to a quantitative baseline.

One last example is of a more traditional scatter plot but with a twist. Here, a group of statisticians were explaining a mathematical tool called K-Means Clustering. Not an easy concept to grasp, like most statistics concepts, but they did it brilliantly. Earlier in the presentation they had shown a video in which M&M sweets changed colour and clustered together, and this explained the basic theory but now they wanted to do a practical demonstration. So they chose a topic close to many people's hearts – beer – and looked at the correlation between alcohol percentage (ABV) and the price-per-litre of a range of different beers. The graph they drew is shown below.

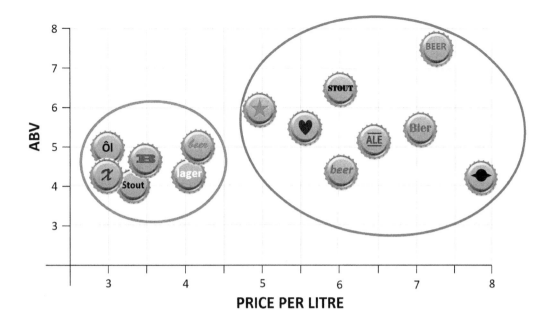

A creative infographic based on an audience-centred, real-world sample.

As you can see, instead of each data-point just being a dot, they drew in the logos of each beer on bottle caps – these have been changed in the above figure for copyright reasons – as these would be familiar to the audience. They also made sure to place the centre-point of each logo at its precise numerical location. Then they ran their algorithm and produced and explained the clusters formed. I understood it perfectly and it was amazing to me that I could grasp an advanced statistics concept in just six minutes having understood precisely nothing that we 'covered' in the year-long statistics courses I did in college. The graph really helped.

You would be well advised in a presentation to keep your graphs simple. But with big screens, bright projectors, images, animations, verbal signposting and enthusiasm, you can do more with the much-maligned graph in a presentation than you can in any other setting. Often graphs are the worst thing in a presentation but they can also be, with a little imagination, the best.

CHAPTER 11

A Distinct Lack of Urgency

The Problem

There is a lack of urgency around presentations. People will spend weeks writing a document – a business plan, a funding proposal, a prospectus – but when it comes to the presentation, they will say things like, 'I fly in the night before, so I'll have time to pull some slides together on the plane.' In regard to all the things we have discussed – stories, infographics, analogies, videos, examples, demonstrations, images – where will you find these on a 90-minute flight to Brussels? In the seat pocket in front of you? Come on! All you get from this kind of 'preparation' is bullet points, which are really just notes-to-self.

You have to scope out a presentation, analyse your audience, create and select ideas, run them past others, fine-tune them, practice them, get stuff ready for the day, get yourself ready for the day, and get there early on the day. Although a presentation is essentially you just talking, and although the naturalness of 'just talking' is the best thing about it, like anything of quality, it has to be produced. Which takes time. Mind you, it doesn't take *that* much time and it is certainly time well spent.

As well as shoddy preparation, people also demonstrate this lack of urgency in delivery. At a recent presentation I attended, the opening line was: 'I'm not going to tell you anything today that you haven't heard before.' Great! Why are you telling us, then? This is no different from the owner of a restaurant leaning over your table and saying, 'I wouldn't eat that if I were you.'

Delivery also lacks urgency when the presentation is scripted, which many are. I got this email, last year, from a guy who had formerly taken one of my courses.

Barry, I just had a speech from a senior manager who at one point looked down at his sheet of paper to read out the words "I really care about..."

Inspiring stuff. It makes me wonder, again, has a presenter ever read anything out that excited anybody? Politicians learn speeches, of course, but they deliver them as if they haven't learnt them, as if they are being earnest and passionate. Why not just be earnest and passionate?

And, of course, the one-size-fits-all stock company presentation is a total urgency drain. I was at one such presentation that ran for 52 minutes and had 31 slides, some with up to 15 bullet points, many with 4-5 thumbnail pictures or graphs. Bad enough, but the slide that really galled me was, 'Typical questions AAA Software – name changed – can help get you an answer for,' and there were eleven of these, in bullet point format, of course. But we weren't seeking answers to 'typical questions', we were seeking answers to specific questions, *our* questions.

You need to make the audience sit up and take notice. Ask yourself
the question: 'why should they care about this?'

This presentation really intrigued me. It was a conference call to a contractor who was presenting modelling software to an engineering client. Myself and a colleague had a connection with the work and were sitting in on the call. The license cost around €30k initially, with annual maintenance of €5k. In other words, it wasn't just McAfee. And yet we got this catch-all – catch-nobody – encyclopaedic presentation with just the date and the client's name changed on the title slide. You wouldn't buy a packet of crayons in a shop if you didn't like the shop assistant or if the stock was flung about the place, so how could this contractor think we were going to pay €30k for their product based on this rubbish? There is something about a presentation that leads people to switch off their common sense and display a total lack of urgency.

The world is a competitive place. Whatever you're trying to do there's always someone doing it already, or on a bigger scale, or with a slicker website, or with longer opening hours, or with offices in more countries, or with more active social media, or with younger, better looking staff. But despite the dizzying, ever-accelerating pace of the modern world, one thing you needn't be intimidated by is the standard of other people's presentations. Most of them are awful, largely due to a lack of effort. Aside of all the things we have discussed in this book – the refusal to tell stories, the fixation with PowerPoint, the curse of knowledge, the reluctance to engage the audience – at a basic level of urgency, most people's presentations fall way short.

Why?

In some ways it's the most interesting question of all.

The Reason

There are two issues here but one masks the other. The obvious reason is fear. Or 'nerves' or 'caution' or whatever you want to call it. It seems counter-intuitive that something that agitates you and makes you sweat, can rob you of urgency; but if you look at the urgency-deficient behaviours outlined above, they can all be traced back to fear.

Presenters apologise in an effort to reduce the gap between themselves and their audience. They read from a script or from their slides so they won't get lost. They use stock company presentations to reduce uncertainty and avoid making braver choices about content. They are *told* to use stock company presentations to reduce uncertainty about what message the company is communicating, which is precisely no message at all, by the way. They show very little imagination or even common sense because that would make their presentations different from everyone else's. They spend very little time preparing – or even thinking about – their upcoming presentations because it's less unpleasant that way and, sure, that's what everyone else does. So, in many insidious ways, fear paralyses and inhibits more than it energises.

Except fear is not the real problem. Fear is actually a mask that prevents you from seeing the real problem. The real problem is that you're not thinking about your audience, not seeing things from their point of view at all. Fear makes you so self-obsessed and inward looking, that it can be hard to spot this. But if you thought about it from the audience's point of view for one second, you would never display such an insulting lack of urgency.

The intense self-consciousness that nerves invoke leads presenters to take their eye off the ball and fail to focus on the audience.

On my desk, as I type, is a parcel containing four inkjet printer cartridges. They are the ones I ordered – two black, one cyan, one yellow – the packaging seems to be intact and the part numbers correspond to the printer I have. So what? Well, what if I only got three cartridges instead of four, and all were magenta? And what if the packaging was torn and there was ink dribbling out of one of the cartridges? And what if the price on the invoice was double what it should have been?

Faced with this scenario you would probably be quite annoyed, if not incensed. But many, it not most, presentations are just like this. There is information but no insight and no real takeaway for the audience, which is just like shipping the wrong parts. There are blurred images, incomprehensible graphs and far too much text, which is just like shipping soiled goods. And at the end, the presenter says something really dumb like, 'I'm sorry for going over time,' or 'I'm sorry the slides were a bit hard to read,' which doubles the insult like doubling the charge on the invoice. You wouldn't do it to a customer with a product, so why do it with a presentation?

The problem is that presenters don't think of their presentation as a product or their audience as a customer. They don't think about their audience, full-stop. They are too preoccupied with themselves. But as I said in chapter 5, presentations fail not because the speaker can't speak but because the audience can't listen, because what is being presented to them is incomprehensible or just plain useless. If you prepare something worth listening to, you will have content you can be urgent about.

The Solution

Simple: do all of the things in this book with energy and interest. Look like you care. Actually care. Prepare with urgency; deliver with urgency. At the risk of repeating myself, I'll sum up everything in seven simple steps:

1. Analyse your audience and figure out what valuable insight you can give them – think: 'expert' & 'interested group' – figure out the next step in the communication chain.
2. Set an aim.
3. Use communication tools such as stories, examples, analogies, demonstrations, images, graphs and videos.
4. Prepare and practise thoroughly.
5. Converse with your audience.
6. Look at your audience.
7. Listen to your audience.

And enjoy it. Done well – and despite a great many dismal counter-examples – there is no better way to grab people than with a presentation. And it is, as I've said many times, as easy as having a chat with a friend.

- End -

The Laurel and Hardy Legacy: Sitcom Stars Talk Stan and Ollie by Barry Brophy

Laurel and Hardy are one of the finest comedy acts to have graced our screens. From their Foreign Legion campaign in *Beau Hunks* to their improvised song and dance routines in *Way Out West*, their comic genius is known, loved, and celebrated by viewers of all ages across the world. In turn, their influence on other comedies has been profound. British sitcoms abound with Oliver-Hardy-like idiots – who don't realise they're idiots – such as: David Brent, Basil Fawlty, Harold Steptoe and Father Ted; as well as their Stan-Laurel-like sidekicks: Gareth Keenan, Manuel, Albert Steptoe and Dougal.

Many people in comedy today are heavily influenced by a black-and-white double-act who made their best films 80 years ago. The *Laurel and Hardy Legacy* traces the impact of Stan and Ollie, and offers reflective insights into fundamental comedy questions. Why were Laurel and Hardy's features not as good as their shorts, and why are film versions of sitcoms never as good as the originals? Why do sitcoms have studio audiences and how did Laurel and Hardy fine-tune their films for the cinema audiences they couldn't see? Why do actors like Oliver Hardy, not comedians, so often play the lead roles in sitcoms?

Based on a series of exclusive interviews with some of the top comic actors and writers of the last 30 years, this book looks at the immense comic legacy of Laurel and Hardy. Stephen Merchant, Richard Wilson, Bruce Forsyth, Ray Galton and Alan Simpson, Tony Robinson, Barry Cryer, Ardal O'Hanlon, Graham Linehan, John Dunsworth, Nigel Planer and Andrew Sachs all talk about their love of Laurel and Hardy and how they influenced their own work. From *Blackadder* and *The Young Ones*, to *Hancock's Half-Hour* and *One Foot in the Grave*, The *Laurel and Hardy Legacy* is a fascinating insight into the hidden workings of comedy.

Write From The Start: The Beginner's Guide to Writing Professional Non-Fiction by Caroline Foster

Do you want to become a writer? Would you like to earn money from writing? Do you know where to begin?

Help is at hand with *Write From The Start* – a practical must-read resource for newcomers to the world of non-fiction writing. It is a vast genre that encompasses books, newspaper and magazine articles, press releases, business copy, the web, blogging, and much more besides.

Jam-packed with great advice, the book is aimed at novice writers, hobbyist writers, or those considering a full-time writing career, and offers a comprehensive guide to help you plan, prepare, and professionally submit your non-fiction work. It is designed to get you up-and-running fast.

Write From The Start will teach you how to explore topic areas methodically, tailor content for different audiences, and create compelling copy. It will teach you which writing styles work best for specific publications, how to improve your chances of securing both commissioned and uncommissioned work, how to build a portfolio that gets results, and how to take that book idea all the way to publication.

Comprised of 16 chapters, there is information on conducting effective research, book submissions, writing for business, copyright and plagiarism pitfalls, formatting, professional support networks, contracts and agreements, the value of humour, ghostwriting, and much more…

By the end of this book – full of practical advice and proven results – you will be well on your path to writing success!

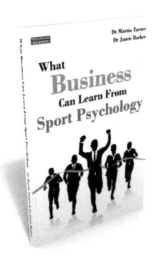

What Business Can Learn From Sport Psychology: Ten Lessons for Peak Professional Performance by Martin Turner & Jamie Barker

"You don't understand anything until you learn it more than one way." Marvin Minsky

How are the best athletes in the world able to function under the immense pressure of competition? By harnessing the potential of their minds to train smart, stay committed, focus, and deliver winning performances with body and mind when the time is right.

The mental side of performance has always been a crucial component for success – but nowadays coaches, teams, and athletes of all levels and abilities are using sport psychology to help fulfil their potential and serve up success.

It goes without saying that business performance has many parallels with sporting performance. But did you realize that the scientific principles of sport psychology, used by elite athletes the world over, are being used by some of the most successful business professionals? Performance – in any context – is about utilizing and deploying every possible resource to fulfil your potential.

This book is about getting into a winning state of body and mind for your performance – whatever that might be – sales pitches, presentations, leadership, strategic thinking, delivery, and more.

In *What Business Can Learn From Sport Psychology* you will develop the most important weapon you need to succeed in business: your mental approach to performance. This book reveals the secrets of the winning mind by exploring the strategies and techniques used by the most successful athletes and professionals on the planet.

As you read this book you will learn about practical and powerful techniques and refine your mental approach to business performance. Based on decades of scientific research, the authors' professional experiences, and the experiences of winning athletes and business professionals, this book is a practical and evidence-driven resource that will teach you how to deal with pressure, break through adversity, embrace challenges, project business confidence, and much more.

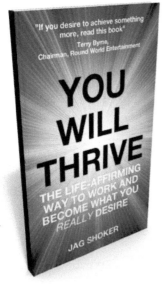

You Will Thrive: The Life-Affirming Way to Work and Become What You Really Desire by Jag Shoker

Have you lost your spark or the passion for what you do? Is your heart no longer in your work or (like so many people) are you simply disillusioned by the frantic race to get ahead in life? Your sense of unease may be getting harder to ignore, and comes from the growing urge to step off the treadmill and pursue a more thrilling *and* meaningful direction in life.

You Will Thrive addresses the subject of modern disillusionment. It is essential reading for people looking to make the most of their talents and be something more in life. Something that matters. Something that makes a difference in the world. Through six empowering steps, it reveals 'the Way' to boldly follow your heart as it leads you to the perfect opportunities you seek. Through every step, it urges you to put a compelling thought to the test:

You possess the power within you to attract the right people, opportunities, and circumstances that you need to become what you desire.

As you'll discover, if you find the *faith* to act on this power and do the Work required to realise your dream, a testing yet life-affirming path will unfold before you as life *orchestrates* the Way to make it all happen.

Jag Shoker is a leading performance coach to high profile business leaders and sports professionals and the author of The 7 Masters Moves of Success. In You Will Thrive he calls upon his own remarkable experience of following the Way and his years of experience in helping others to pursue it to much greater effect.

*

See all our books at: http://www.bennionkearny.com/books/